SERMON ILLUSTRATIONS FOR THE GOSPEL LESSONS

Footprints

One night a man had a dream. He dreamed he was walking along the beach with the Lord. Across the sky flashed scenes from his life. For each scene, he noticed two sets of footprints in the sand: one belonging to him, and the other to the Lord.

When the last scene of his life flashed before him, he looked back at the footprints in the sand. He noticed that many times along the path of his life there was only one set of footprints. He also noticed that it happened at the very lowest and saddest times in his life.

This really bothered him and he questioned the Lord about it.

"Lord, you said that once I decided to follow you, you'd walk with me all the way. But I have noticed that during the most troublesome times in my life, there is only one set of footprints.

I don't understand why when I needed you the most you would leave me.

The Lord replied, "My son, My precious child, I love you and would never leave you. During your times of trial and suffering, when you see only one set of footprints, it was then that I carried you."

Author unknown

THIS BOOK BELONGS TO

Jerry Borkowsky

Publishing House
St. Louis

Copyright © 1980, 1981, and 1982 Concordia Publishing House
3558 South Jefferson Avenue, St. Louis, MO 63118

Manufactured in the United States of America

Library of Congress Cataloging in Publication Data

Main entry under title:
Sermon Illustrations for the Gospel lessons.

    1. Homiletical illustrations.
BV4225.2.S44 1983   251'.08   82-18261
ISBN 0-570-03875-8

---

1 2 3 4 5 6 7 8 9 10   WP   92 91 90 89 88 87 86 85 84 83

Preface

Preachers can never have too many windows in their sermons, as illustrations have been called. One good illustration is often worth the price of a whole sermon.

To assist the preacher who uses the three-year lectionary, Concordia Publishing House has gathered the illustrations published as bonus booklets for the *Concordia Pulpit* 1981, 1982, and 1983 into one volume, providing at least one illustration or quotation for each of the Gospel texts in Series A, B, and C.

Documentation as to source has been provided wherever possible. Illustrations signed by a contributor are taken to be original.

Scripture and topical indexes for each series are found at the end of each set of illustrations, thus serving as references for those not following the three-year lectionary as well as for those who do.

May these illustrations enrich and make more effective the proclamation of the divine story of grace and redemption.

—The Publisher

Gospel Lessons, Series A

by
RICHARD ANDERSEN and DONALD DEFFNER

Contributors

First Sunday in Advent Through Good Friday—Dr. Richard Andersen
Easter Sunday Through Reformation—Dr. Donald L. Deffner

Sources—Series A

The Pyramids and Sphinx by Desmond Stewart, Newsweek Book Division, New York, 1971.
Complete Stories of the Great Operas, Milton Cross, Doubleday, 1947.
Proclamation, Series A, Epiphany, by Merrill R. Abbey, Fortress Press, 1974.
Demian by Hermann Hesse, Harper & Row, New York, 1965.
The Hammer of God by Bo Giertz, Augsburg Publishing House, 1973.
Living Lenten Portraits by Richard Andersen, Concordia, St. Louis, 1975.
One Hundred Great Lives by John Allen, Greystone Press, New York, 1944.
"Is There a Doctor in the House?" Time magazine, June 4, 1970.
Funny, You Don't Look Christian, Weybright and Talley, Inc.
The Strong-Willed Child by James Dobson, Tyndale House Publishers.
Each New Day by Corrie ten Boom, World Wide Publications.
Newsletter, First Immanuel Lutheran Church, San Jose, CA, April 1977.
The Becomers by Keith Miller, Word Books.
Loyalty Christ and Country by Edmund A. Puseman, April 1978.
Tramp for the Lord by Corrie ten Boom, Pillar Books.
Bulletin, Roman Catholic Church, Boyne Falls, MI, September 1977.
The Age and You by Alvin N. Rogness, Augsburg Publishing House.
Jesus Christ, Our Hope by Walter A. Maier, Concordia.
What Luther Says by Ewald Plass, Concordia, 1959, I, p. 496.
Children and the Bible by Ethel L. Smither, Abingdon.
What Luther Says by Ewald Plass, Concordia, 1959, II, p. 954.
Beyond Personality by C. S. Lewis, Macmillan.
Life Together by Dietrich Bonhoeffer, Harper & Row.
"What Do You Know by Heart?" by Henri J. M. Nouwen, *Sojourners,* August 1977.
Trinity Trumpet, Trinity Lutheran Church, Walnut Creek, CA, January 1978.
Unity News, Unity Lutheran Church, Bel Nor, MO, October 27, 1977.

The First Sunday in Advent   *Palm Sunday*

MATTHEW 21:1-11

Caesar entered Rome with his chariot drawn by six tawny lions; Pompey used elephants to pull his, while other Roman emperors came riding golden chariots led by six or eight magnificent stallions. Kaiser Wilhelm II had hoped to have the streets of Jerusalem widened so that he might enter in a gilded carriage; the best that could be done was to heighten the Jaffa Gate so that he could come in on horseback to the dedication of the Lutheran Church of the Redeemer.

Hitler wanted to parade triumphantly into Paris after its fall, but his adjutants discouraged him from doing so. However, his General von Bock, chief of Army Group B, reached the city *before* his troops, and took the salute of the first combat troops. Arches and columns, plaques and memorials have long heralded the historical entry of great conquerors and resplendent kings. With Jesus, it was a donkey. A little fanfare, but hardly a triumph. What was to be His triumph was what others would consider His defeat. So Advent begins. A little fanfare, but hardly a triumph. The victory lies yet ahead.

—From various sources
The Great Cities: Jerusalem (Time/Life)
Inside the Third Reich, Albert Speer
Adoph Hitler, John Toland
Beautiful Possibilities for Today, Robert H. Schuller

The Second Sunday in Advent   *Baptism/Holy Spirit*

MATTHEW 3:1-12

The QE2 (the Cunard liner, *Queen Elizabeth II*) gets nowhere without water. Similarly, it is the repentant and baptized Christian who goes from standstill to steady-as-she-goes as grace bouys him up. But what sends the QE2 at record-breaking speed across the Seven Seas is oil-fired boilers. Christians move very little in spiritual growth until the fire of the Spirit makes them zoom at full-speed-ahead.

The Third Sunday in Advent *Doubt/Faith*

MATTHEW 11:2-11

David Roberts has said that once he heard a man confess, "I spent twenty years trying to come to terms with my doubts. Then one day it dawned on me that I had better come to terms with my faith."

When people shift from doubt to faith they make scientific discoveries as Curie and Salk; they land on the moon and take pictures of Mars and Saturn with orbiting cameras; they limit the manufacture of armaments as in the SALT negotiations, and sue for peace as Israel and Egypt have done. But such a shift is not without its questions. John the Baptist asked his. And Jesus cataloged the ready evidence.

When the Chinese put their doubts behind them, they built the Great Wall of China during the reign of Emperor Ch'in Shih Huang Ti in 228 B.C.; and the followers of John went away confident in the truth they found in Jesus.

The Fourth Sunday in Advent *Marriage*

MATTHEW 1:18-25

The problem of pregnancy out-of-wedlock proved ticklish to the Holy Family for a time. The appearance of an angel of the Lord in a dream provided Joseph with something more than a resolve to divorce Mary quietly.

In a Jan. 15, 1979, series of articles on the state of marriage in California, the Los Angeles *Times* listed clues to a happy marriage provided by UCLA psychologist Michael Goldstein. Among them were these: Agreement on fundamental values about life, and a willingness to fight through problems in a mature way, as well as mutual support. Were these not assured by the angel, so that Joseph could move into marriage without reservations?

In the United States in 1977, there were 2,176,000 marriages performed, and 1,097,000 divorces decreed. A little prayerful dreaming might have forestalled the latter, and a search for the clues to a possibly happy marriage might have tightened the hope for the former.

—Statistics from the 1979 *Reader's Digest Almanac and Yearbook*

The Nativity of Our Lord *Complacency/Faith*
Christmas Day

LUKE 2:1-20

Soren Kierkegaard, a century ago, used this illustration in objection to complacency. Suppose, he suggested, there was a community of geese; they could talk, and every seventh day they gathered for a service. One gander would preach, and tell of their lofty destiny, the Creator's high goal for them, and how, by the use of their wings they could fly to distant regions where they were meant actually to live.

Waddling home, the geese could begin to eat the farmer's grain, paying no attention to the message preached. They would begin to talk about what ugly things might take place if they took the sermon too seriously. They would tell of how one, who made full use of the wings the Creator had given him had met with an awful fate. Sunday after Sunday, they gathered solemnly, but during the week they were content to remain in the barnyard. There they grew plump and delicate . . . just right for the holiday table.

The shepherds were wiser. They spread the Good News of Jesus' birth. They took to heart the lofty destiny the angels' song acclaimed.

—Material from W. Rowry in *Kierkegaard,* 1957

The First Sunday After Christmas   *Flight (Jesus') to Egypt*

MATTHEW 2:13-15, 19-23

Legends abound about Jesus. Why did He have to flee, to hide?

The Egyptian Christians trace the advent of the Holy Family as refugees into their land: they entered the country at the El Kantara frontier post, Joseph and Mary, Jesus, a midwife, and donkey. Gaius Turranius was the governor of the Roman province. They followed the Sinai road used by the Hyksos, the Hebrew patriarchs, and Alexander's army. They headed for Babylon-in-Egypt at the neck of the delta where Joseph was to sell the gifts of the Magi to finance their travels deep into Upper Egypt. In going past Heliopolis, they approached the fresh-water spring known as the Source of the Sun, and there, the legend continues, "prodigious happenings in this center of Re worship" took place. Gigantic statues of Ptah, Thoth, Osiris, and Isis "crashed to the ground in spontaneous homage to incarnate truth."

Scripture's silence about the Egyptian sojourn does not obscure its divine fore-plan, nor does it hide the reality that flight at times is a positive recourse. It does fuel imagination, however, but the truth remains.

—*The Pyramids and Sphinx* by Desmond Stewart
Newsweek Book Division, New York, 1971

The Second Sunday After Christmas   *Comfort/Security*

JOHN 1:1-18

Some years ago while traveling along the California coast, my family and I stopped for a brief rest by a gleaming lighthouse manned by the Coast Guard. We took several pictures of the handsome structure, but we were unable to enter. A guard told us it was off limits. Bombarded with questions from the children, the young man explained the operation of the great beacon. He was not the light, but he bore witness to it.

As the fog began to roll steadily on shore, we became aware that the light was functioning, and had been for some time. It was as one particular sweep of the lamp brightened the dark, billowing fog that I realized the graphic meaning of John's words, "The true light that enlightens every man was coming into the world. He was in the world, and the world was made through Him, yet the world knew Him not." I could imagine ships distressed at sea finding comfort in such a beacon, and the little ark of my life, launched upon destiny's deep sea, finds comfort yet in the "true light that enlightens every man."

The Epiphany of Our Lord   *Star/Light*

MATTHEW 2:1-12

An Associated Press story dated Dec. 25, 1978, tells of new-found evidence that the planet Jupiter, shining like a star, appeared directly over Bethlehem on December 25 in the year 2 B.C. Dr. Ernest L. Martin, director of the Foundation for Biblical Research in

Pasadena, says that for six days, the shining planet appeared to be stationary, which was caused by the earth moving away from and traveling faster than Jupiter.

A UPI story of Dec. 26, 1978, says another astronomer, who is also an assistant professor of physics at the University of Missouri—Columbia, Dr. Charles Peterson, says a "star" as luminous as the mysterious Star of Bethlehem may apepar in 1982.

There are other plausible possibilities to account for the star, say some, but it was not the heavenly body that was the real *star* of that astral wonder. It was and is Jesus. Bright stars come and go. Jesus shines forever.

The Baptism of Our Lord (First Sunday After the Epiphany) *Holy Spirit/Pentecost*

MATTHEW 3:13-17

Doves have long been messengers. Noah utilized a dove to discover if the waters had subsided following the Flood (Gen. 8:8, 10). It is not surprising that God Himself should choose the imagery of the dove by which to descend and bless the Baptism of His Son through the appearance of the Holy Spirit.

In the early days of news gatherings, Reuters used pigeons to report the latest events of the French Revolution to German newspapers (1849).

It was, however, the echo of the fluttering wings of the Dove of the Spirit that Richard Strauss incorporated into his opera, *Salome,* the story based on the Oscar Wilde dramatic poem, which took its inspiration from the Scriptures, that reminds us of the message of divine blessing that occurred at the Lord's Baptism. Twice in the great dramatic score, Herod hears the sound of rushing wind, and gasps "that mighty wings are beating in the air around him." Pentecost has the same awesome echo.

To the faithful, the message of the Dove is peace. To the unbelieving, it is a fearsome message of Divine wrath.

—Encyclopaedia Britannica
—Complete Stories of the Great Operas, Milton Cross, Doubleday, 1947

Second Sunday After the Epiphany *Atonement*

JOHN 1:29-41

Oscar Wilde's poetic play dramatizes the last hours of the life of John the Baptist. In the Richard Strauss opera, *Salome,* Jokanaan (John the Baptist) is confined to a dungeon that is beneath the terrace of Herod's palace. Narraboth, a young Syrian captain of the guard, "looks with burning eyes toward the banquet hall, where Salome," Herodias' daughter, is feasting with Herod and his court.

Suddenly from the depths of the dungeon comes the penetrating voice of Jokanaan, intoning, "Nach mir wird Einer kommen der ist starker als ich (After me cometh One mightier than I)." It is the message he seeks to impart to the infatuated and foolish Salome, and likewise to Herod. It is the message generations have ignored, but it remains the truth. Christ has come as the Sacrificial Lamb, the Messiah, to not only vindicate John's death, but atone for sin and mightily destroy the barrier between God and man. Life is not a staged opera; therefore the dramatic words of the Baptizer are not to be dismissed as with the fall of a curtain.

—Complete Stories of the Great Operas, Milton Cross, Doubleday, 1974

The Third Sunday After the Epiphany   *Evangelism*

MATTHEW 4:12-23

When Dorothy took to the Yellow Brick Road on the way to the Land of Oz, she discipled a tin man, a cowardly lion, and a straw-stuffed scarecrow by inspiring them with hope, cajoling them with kindness, and simply by the sparkle of personality, her charisma. By the time she got to Emerald City, she captured the fancy of the wizard and charmed the whimsy of the populace.

For Dorothy, fishing for men was simpler than fishing for fish.

Jesus had demonstrated that a crowd will always follow someone of conviction. Adolph Hilter, Idi Amin, and Jim Jones exploited that concept. The commercial world has made it its hallmark, huckstering candidates and canned goods by cleverly casting nets to catch the unwary and the unknowing. Japanese and Russian fishing trawlers have the same questionable ethics, while the average Christian has learned little from the Lord's approach.

To be a fisher of men who succeeds, if not with all at least with many, remember how the Lord has phrased His promise to the disciples: "Follow *me*," and *I* will *make* you fishers of men." Technique can never supplant power.

The Fourth Sunday After the Epiphany   *Power*

MATTHEW 5:1-12

"In a one-act play, *The Terrible Meek*, Charles Rann Kennedy contrasts the imperial power of Rome with the ultimately prevailing power of Jesus. The scene is the hill of crucifixion; the struggle rages within the mind and will of the centurion in charge of the execution. Forced to choose between the two kinds of power brought to issue on that hill, he concludes that what Jesus has exemplified 'will shake all the empires and kingdoms of the world into the dust.' Jesus and His true followers, he says, are 'the terrible meek, the fierce, agonizing meek.'"

—Merrill R. Abbey in *Proclamation, Series A*, Epiphany, Fortress Press, 1974

The Fifth Sunday After the Epiphany   *Faith/Stewardship*

MATTHEW 5:13-20

Salt had a value in ancient times that we fail to comprehend today:
—covenants were sealed with salt (Num. 18:19) . . . hence a "covenant of salt"
—use of salt was a bond of fidelity (i.e., the Arab expression "there is salt between us")
—salt that had lost its savor was earthly residuum with little taste because the
    sodium chloride had been rinsed out, hence the Persian phrase "untrue to salt" or
    disloyal, ungrateful.
—many ancient roads were built to accommodate the desire for salt:
    . . . the Via Salaria in Italy between the salt pans of Ostia and the Sabine
    . . . Herodotus speaks of the caravan route uniting the salt oases of Libya
    . . . the trade route between the Aegean and the coasts of southern Russia
—cakes of salt were used as money in Abyssinia and Tibet and Rome

When Jesus said "You are the salt of the earth, . . ." He was saying you have value like a binding contract, money in the bank, and the whole structure of human commerce. Faith is even more important than salt, for faith bridges the separation to eternity. Let it not lose its savor.

—material from Encyclopaedia Brittanica

The Sixth Sunday After the Epiphany   *Faith/Good Works*

MATTHEW 5:20-37

Saving faith does not look at its own works. (Saving faith) is the sort of faith that does not look at its works nor at its own strength and worthiness, noting what sort of *qualitas* or newly created or infused virtue it may be, lying in the heart, as the blind sophists dream and pretend. But faith goes out of itself, clings to Christ, and embraces Him as its own possession; and faith is certain that it is loved by God for His sake and not for the sake of its own works, worthiness, or merit.

—What Luther Says, Ewald Plass,
Concordia, St. Louis, 1959, Vol. I, p. 496).

The Seventh Sunday After the Epiphany   *Temptation*

MATTHEW 5:38-48

Jesus urges us "not to resist one who is evil." The implication is that we're not to succumb to the powers of an evil person, nor are we to resist him with violence, but love.

Young Emil Sinclair, as yet unconfirmed, and wrestling with a growing faith taunted by spiritual uncertainties, boasts of a minor infraction to a neighborhood bully in Hermann Hesse's novel *Demian*. Emil "had stolen a whole sackful of apples one night, and by no means ordinary apples, but apples of the very best sort."

Franz Kromer, the bully, saw a chance for profit and to keep quiet used the confession as a tool to extort money from the youngster. Sinclair did not resist, and the incident plagued him the rest of his life. Violence was not called for, but love was. Love of neighbor means calling people to honor and honesty. That is not to resist *them* and their need but, as St. Peter enjoins us, to resist the *the adversary* who prowls around like a roaring lion—and in the face of temptation be firm in faith (1 Peter 5:9). Loving "one who is evil" is to hate any evil actions while motivating the person to fulfill his/her potential for good.

—Reference to Demian by Hermann Hesse, Harper & Row, New York, 1965

The Transfiguration of Our Lord   *Repentance/Faith/Grace*
The Last Sunday After the Epiphany

MATTHEW 17:1-9

(The retired Lutheran bishop of Gothenburg, Sweden, the Rt. Rev. Bo Giertz, wrote a number of novels that were useful in the deepening of the faith of his diocese. *The Hammer of God* tells the story of a Swedish parish at three distinct periods in its life.)

The parish curate was assigned to preach on Transfiguration Day, but before he had completed preparations for his sermon, he was called out to minister to a dying man a considerable distance from the rectory. It was a long, arduous trip by horse, and when he

12

returned the next morning, he arrived barely in time for the worship service. Grabbing a copy of Schartau's *Fifteen Sermons,* he turned to a message based on Matthew 17:1-9 and began to read from the pulpit.

"'It is a blessed thing when a believing soul looks in the Word for Jesus only,' he read.

"That I have not done, thought Fridfeldt. I have looked for penitence, for amendment of life. I have taken stock of my deeds, but I have lost sight of Jesus in all this mess.

"Like hammer blows aimed with unerring precision against the head of a nail, the words 'Jesus only,' recurred again and again and sank ever deeper into the consciousness. *Jesus only,* the foundation of faith, and man sees nothing else, believes in nothing else, builds his hope on nothing else, when through the awakening he has had his eyes opened to see his state of corruption and condemnation."

As he preached, the transfiguring power found a receptive heart in the curate. His battle in understanding sin and grace was resolved. Here was the solution: "sin always remaining, yet always atoned for." Jesus only is the answer now and always.

—*The Hammer of God* by Bo Giertz, Augsburg Paperback, 1973, Minneapolis

Ash Wednesday   *Serving/Prayer*

MATTHEW 6:1-6, 16-21

She is a Roman Catholic lay theologian, a Mexican living in Cuernavaca, who told her story quietly over an evening meal in a Sacramento hotel. Yolanda de Lallande told of her remarkable efforts to help the lepers of Mexico City. She literally broke her back four times, necessitating painful surgery and extended periods of agony on the Stryker bed, because she carried 50 kilo sacks of beans and rice to the lepers in a colony on the outskirts of the city over several years.

No one would minister to them. No priests would come to attend the dying. No doctors would go. No nurses. No social workers. After three years, she burst into the office of the Minister of Health and demanded help for the poor wretches living in the filth and squalor of an abominable existence. It was discovered that innumerable people were stealing from the lepers everything to which they were entitled. Fifteen went to jail because of their theft of food, medicines, and aid.

Senora Lallande went to minister to the lepers because no one else would. She went in devotion to Christ. It was a ministry of prayer lived out in feeding the hungry and visiting the poor. She found a bank filled with living jewels that others had neglected and ignored, a treasure house of gems that God used and cleaned and polished through her. Her piety was not practiced *before* men, but like Jesus, *on* mankind.

The First Sunday in Lent   *Christian Life/Goals*

MATTHEW 4:1-11

It seems impossible.

"You shall worship the Lord your God and Him only shall you serve," said Jesus as He dismissed the Tempter during those trying forty days in the wilderness.

It is Don Quixote, the idealist, who sings in *Man of La Mancha* "The Impossible Dream," charting the quest that's his "to follow that star, No matter how hopeless, no matter how far." It's the Mother Abbess in the *Sound of Music* who encourages Maria to find her dream, "A dream that will need all the love you can give Every day of your life for as

13

long as you live." She tells her to climb every mountain, to search high and low, to follow every byway, every path she knows. Eliza Doolittle, in her quest for a fantastic future, sees it as a room somewhere, far away from the cold night air; with one enormous chair. She asks, "Oh, wouldn't it be loverly?" *My Fair Lady's* miracle is a flower-seller who is turned into an amazing butterfly, one thought to be of royal blood, but who remains merely Eliza Doolittle of the London slums.

What characters of musical comedies communicate is the positive possibility of achieving their objectives. It is far more real than fantasy. Every invention, every cure for a disease, every great work of art began as a hope, a dream, a potential, a goal. So it is with the commendation of our Lord. To worship the Lord only and serve Him solely is to have more than an impossible dream—but a joyous reality.

The Second Sunday in Lent   *Jesus/Worship*

JOHN 4:5-26 (27-30, 39-42)

There is the temptation to commemorate a revelatory experience by building monuments.
—the Holy Land is marked with such places every few feet it seems;
—the Wartburg, where Luther tossed an inkpot at the devil, and the spot in Worms where Luther stood his ground before the Emperor's diet are pointed out;
—where Brigham Young said, "This is the place," and built the Mormon settlement at Salt Lake City is to be found a lofty memorial;
—Lourdes and Fatima and countless other shrines are popular in the Roman Catholic world.

When Jesus told the Samaritan woman that "the hour is coming when neither on this mountain nor in Jerusalem will you worship the Father," He was intimating that the monumental temples of the Samaritans and Jews are superseded by an attitude. Worship is not granite and marble monuments with gold leaf and pointed arches. "God is spirit, and those who worship Him must worship in spirit and truth," He said.

Historical remembrance is one thing, but worship that is truly alive worships a *living* God. The woman at the well met Him, and the well has become even more famous because of it. It was the experience, not the well; and the Messianic revelation, and not the occasion that is truly memorable. It is, after all, the water in the well, and not the wellhouse that is of importance. It is Jesus Himself who wells up to eternal life.

The Third Sunday in Lent   *Sight/Faith*

JOHN 9:1-41

Bartimaeus speaks:
"Most of you will forget.... You will think of me as some phenomenon of nature, rather than the blind man the Savior healed. You will try to explain away the miracle with some flashy logic to thus innoculate yourself from the faith that saves. But let me give you one last word: When you have lived in the squalor and filth of poverty; when you have led a visionless life in which you have not seen the flowering of the desert after the winter's abundant rains, or watched children frolic about the neighborhood, or perceived the splendor of brilliant colors . . . an azure sky, a snow white peak, a crimson rose, or a vermillion sunset . . . when you have been blinded to all of these miracles of God only to

14

experience them in one instant at the Lord Christ's behest, you cannot dismiss Bartimaeus as some fraud of Scripture, some freak of nature. You see him fully to be what he is . . . a sightless man that Jesus loved, and to whom He gave more than a vision of this world in which we live, a man to whom He gave the vision of what it means to believe . . . perhaps blindly . . . yet knowingly.

"Look at me! I can see! I see Jesus as Lord and Savior. I see eternity with Him. What do you see? Or do you see at all?"

—"Bartimaeus" in Living Lenten Portraits, Richard Andersen,
Concordia, St. Louis, 1975

The Fourth Sunday in Lent   *Service/Humility*

MATTHEW 20:17-28

"I have done nothing to make any human being remember that I have lived," wrote Abraham Lincoln at age thirty-two. "Yet what I wish to live for is to connect my name with the events of my day and generation, to link my name with something which will be of interest to my fellow men."

It is not wrong to aspire to high office. It is not even wrong to have others intercede in behalf of competent candidates. What the mother of James and John requested of Jesus in having Him assign the two to sit on either side of Him in the Kingdom was more than arrogant motherly pride. Her sons would be faithful in drinking the cup of Christ, but only the Father could determine who would occupy such positions. Jesus honored that.

Lincoln gained his objective. He became a servant, and in that role the nation elevated him to greatness. But it was the Suffering Servant seen in Jesus that has made His name greater than any human being, who at age thirty-three fulfilled the promise and kept the covenant.

—"Abraham Lincoln," in One Hundred Great Lives by
John Allen; Greystone Press, New York, 1944

The Fifth Sunday in Lent   *Resurrection/Death*

JOHN 11:1-53

Composer Jule Styne believes that great Broadway shows like "My Fair Lady," "Oklahoma," and "Fiddler on the Roof" were great from the start with only a modest amount of polishing needed. However, it took Geoffrey Holder and some intensive surgery to turn a floundering "The Wiz" into a successful trip down the Yellow Brick Road. Six new songs and six new dancers, a new choreographer and a new producer were required to bring Richard Rodgers' "I Remember Mama" to life and then it "bombed." "Funny Girl," we're told, went through forty rewrites of the last scene, and postponed opening night five times, but then Jerome Robbins was brought in, and he breathed fresh life into it. Dying, they were not dead.

You can revive an old show: "No, No, Nanette." You can extend a show's life by some dramatic changes, as when Harold Prince changed "Hello, Dolly" from a white cast to a black one, or when a successful play such as "Auntie Mame" was turned into a musical. You can revive people, or help them correct their problems or undergo drastic surgery to extend life and broaden it. But no one but God can give life to the dead. No producer can produce life. No star can revive a human corpse. New costumes, bright new tunes, a whole chorus line of dancers cannot kick new life into a dead body. But God can. God did. In Christ, God made dry bones to live.

—information based on "Is There a Doctor in the House?" in the June 4, 1979, *Time* magazine

The Sunday of the Passion
Palm Sunday

Palms/Praise

MATTHEW 21:1-11

What good are palms?
Date palms furnish fruit that's tasty and sweet.
The fronds, or branches, were used in making baskets. Rattan palms are used in making furniture, while the fronds are often used to shade individuals and groups in small desert ramadas. You can see them along Arizona highways.
Palm trees provide wax, sugar, oil, tannin, dyestuff, resin, and juice.
For wandering caravaneers, the sight of palm trees meant water. "Welcome," they seemed to say. "Life is here; we mark a well; come rest with us."
What better symbol for Jesus? He, too, is Savior and Lord, providing shade from the devil's abuse, nurturing us with Himself, and signaling the presence of living water.
In France, one of the highest military decorations given is the *Croix de Guerre* ("The Cross of War"), which is given to only the bravest soldiers. Those honored twice or more receive palm branches attached to the original medal. It means not only triumph, but commendation for the way in which it was accomplished. Palms mean praise. Thus the crowd praised Jesus in a way the world hasn't forgotten.

—material from *Encyclopaedia Brittanica*

Maundy Thursday

Uncertainty/Persistence

JOHN 13:1-7, 34

Do you recall the story of how the news was passed along to England concerning Wellington's success at Waterloo? It came by a sailing ship to the south coast of England, and was wigwagged by signal flags to London. When the message reached Winchester, the signaler atop the Cathedral began to spell out the message. "Wellington defeated . . ." he wig-wagged; then fog descended and hid the signals from view. The news went on to London. When the message was read, "Wellington defeated," the whole country was in despair. After awhile, the fog lifted and the signaler atop Winchester Cathedral was still at work completing the message, "t-h-e e-n-e-m-y." The thrilling news raced across the land and lifted all the hearts: "Wellington defeated the enemy."
To those in the Upper Room, the message was unclear, hazed over by uncertainty, but by Easter Day the total signal was received: "Jesus Christ defeated the enemy."

Good Friday

Death/Courage

JOHN 18:1—19:42 or JOHN 19:17-30

At the climax of Nikos Kazantzakis' great novel, "The Greek Passion," a young shepherd boy who was to play the role of Jesus in the village passion play assumes not only the outward appearance of the Lord but an attitude very similar to His. He is about to be sacrificed by the villagers because of their misunderstanding and passionate hatred, not at all dissimilar from the Jerusalem mobs.

"Aren't you afraid?" asked an adversary. "Aren't you afraid of the Agha, of priest Grigoris, of the village?"

"The man who's not afraid of death isn't afraid of anyone, Panayotaros; there's my secret. Let's go!"

Manolios knew the nature of Jesus. He had no fear of men, of the cross, of death or the grave. As St. Paul wrote, "Love bears all things, believes all things, hopes all things, endures all things" (1 Cor. 13:7).

—*The Greek Passion* by Nikos Kazantzakis, Simon and Schuster, 1953

Easter

Easter Joy

MATTHEW 28:1-10

"HA! HA! HA!"

In Tanzania when Christians sing "Alleluia" on Easter morning, they literally laugh at the forces of evil conquered by Christ's resurrection.

"Alleluia! HA! HA! HA!" they shout. "Alleluia! HA! HA! HA!"

That is the real message of Easter—that we can sing with joyous laughter on the day of Christ's victory. For He has burst the bonds of death and by His resurrection has assured us the victory over Satan and death.

Second Sunday of Easter

Easter/Faith

JOHN 20:19-31

An Easter Faith

"Sorrow not . . . as others which have no hope."

Robert M. Herhold tells the story of a cabdriver in Chicago who picked up a woman outside a hospital one night. As the cab pulled away from the curb, the woman broke into tears.

The woman cried for some time. Finally, when the cabdriver stopped for a red light, he turned to her and asked if something rough had just happened back at the hospital.

The woman wiped her eyes and tried to control herself as she replied: "Yes, my mother just died."

After a few more moments of driving, the cabbie asked: "Are you a religious person? A Christian maybe?"

"Well, I go to church regularly," the woman replied.

"What about your mother?" the cabbie asked.

"That I am sure of," the woman replied. "She was the best Christian I have ever known."

To which the cabbie responded: "Lady, then why are you crying as if everything was over?"

—Robert M. Herhold, *Funny, You Don't Look Christian,*
Weybright and Talley, Inc., pp. 66—67).

Third Sunday of Easter   *Unseen Guest*

LUKE 24:13-35

Christ

Some years ago George and Adeline Hohmann founded the Redwood Boys Ranch for underprivileged youth at Napa, Calif. A memorable moment each day was at mealtime when one lad had the privilege of pushing in the one chair left empty at the table. It was the Lord's chair. He was the Unseen Guest at every meal.

Fourth Sunday of Easter   *Life Abundant*

JOHN 10:1-10

That Which Really Satisfies

A middle-aged housewife comments: "I always thought that by the time (my husband) had his own business, we had paid off the mortgage on the house, and the kids were old enough to look after themselves, that I'd be home safe. I thought there'd be no more problems. But it hasn't worked out that way. I worked hard, and I got most of the things I wanted, but they don't seem to mean what I thought they would. I'm getting bored with my life. I even begin to envy those women who have high pressure careers. I have a nice house, but I have spent 15 years in it bringing up two kids, and I'm fed up with it. I'd like to move back into an apartment, like (my husband) and I had when we were first married. These days the two of us seem to spend half our time arguing about what went wrong. We feel as though we wasted a lot of time. But I don't think either of us really knows what we want now—except that it's something else besides what we have."

Fifth Sunday of Easter   *Christ the Way*

JOHN 14:1-12

Following the Boundaries

A man was flying his single-engine airplane towards a small country airport. It was late in the day, and before he could get the plane into position to land, he could not see the hazy field below. He had no lights on his plane and there was no one on duty at the airport. He began circling, but the darkness deepened, and for two hours he flew the plane around and around, knowing that he would certainly crash when his fuel was expended.

Then a miracle occurred. Someone on the ground had heard his engine and realized his plight. A man drove his car back and forth on the runaway, to show where the airstrip was, and then shone the headlights from the far end of the strip to guide the pilot to a safe landing.

Christ is the Light and the Way for our lives. There is safety in the lighted area of His path for us. But disaster lies in the darkness to the left or the right.

—Adapted from a story by James Dobson, *The Strong-Willed Child*,
Tyndale House Publishers, Inc., p. 9

Sixth Sunday of Easter

JOHN 14:15-21

God Is Our Refuge

A great church leader lay dying of a rare disease. His brain was still alert, but he could not speak, and his body was immobile except that he could move a finger or two. As the end neared, the doctors asked him to tap 50 times with his finger to determine if they could still communicate with him.

One day he tapped only 46 times, and they thought he was slipping away. But the next day, and the next, the man's fingers tapped exactly 46 times.

Finally someone brought a Bible and read the first verse of Psalm 46: "God is our refuge and strength, a very present help in trouble."

And as the verse was read, they could tell in his eyes that that was the message he was communicating to them.

The Ascension of our Lord

Witnessing

LUKE 24:44-53

Every Christian a Witness

Rev. Paul Foust in his book *Reborn to Multiply* lists five advantages that a layperson has over a pastor:

1. There are 600 times as many of them.

2. They are where the unbelieving world is, working right beside them.

3. They are more able to stay with the candidate for the Kingdom and follow up.

4. They are satisfied customers while I am a "paid witness," if you will! And you know what juries think of paid witnesses!

5. "Every Christian a witness" is God's system. A pastor's work is to equip the people of God for their witness through sermons, teaching, and by leading and developing evangelism programs.

Seventh Sunday of Easter

God's Plan Completed

JOHN 17:1-11

The Hour Has Come

A construction engineer was once confined to his bed, his legs paralyzed, but because of his reputation for great skill he was asked to draw the blueprints for a great suspension bridge. The plans were at last completed and put into the hands of those who were to do the actual construction.

Months passed by and the bridge was finally finished. Four men came to the engineer's room and carried him out on his cot to a place where he was able to view the bridge spanning a wide river, over which cars and trucks were rapidly passing. Tears filled his eyes, and looking down at the blueprints in his hands, he cried out: "It's just like the plan; it's just like the plan!"

The Day of Pentecost *Pentecost*

JOHN 20:19-23

Filled with the Spirit

"I have a glove here in my hand. The glove cannot do anything by itself, but when my hand is in it, it can do many things. True, it is not the glove, but my hand in the glove that acts. We are gloves. It is the Holy Spirit in us who is the hand, who does the job. We have to make room for the hand so that every finger is filled."

The question on Pentecost is not whether God is blessing our own plans and programs but whether we are open to the great opportunities to which His Spirit calls us.

"Once the Lord said to a faithful evangelist, 'You have been working for Me with the utmost sincerity for seven years. All that time I have been waiting for the moment that I could start to work through you'"

—Corrie ten Boom, Each New Day,
World Wide Publications, devotions for May 15 and 13

The Holy Trinity *The Great Commission*
(First Sunday After Pentecost)

MATTHEW 28:16-20

Sacramentum, the Military Oath

In the world-famous Roman armies, the decisive act of becoming a soldier was called the *sacramentum,* that is, the military oath. The Christian church adopted this word for the decisive act of becoming a soldier of Christ; Baptism, and especially the vows taken at Baptism, were called the *sacramentum.* By becoming a Christian through the *sacramentum,* we cease to be civilians, and we become soldiers actively engaged in Christ's battle for the world. The New Testament and the early church never admitted a distinction between active and passive members.

In churches all over the world, however, the great majority of those who have made the *sacramentum* (baptismal vow) do not actually join in Christ's struggle for the world. After taking "the military oath," many of them become deserters, conforming themselves to the world, and not being transformed by the renewal of their minds (Rom. 12:2). Others go on permanent leave, only returning occasionally to "check in." They lead a double life, following two different sets of ethics—one for their private, Sunday life, and one for their life in the work-a-day world. Still others always remain in the barracks, being more and more knowledgeable about the "spiritual armor of God," but never leaving their Christian camp to fight for the reconciliation of the world. In fact, under these circumstances, it sometimes happens that the only battles in which they engage take place right there in the barracks!

—Newsletter, First Immanuel Lutheran Church, San Jose, CA, April 1977

Second Sunday After Pentecost *Doers, Not Just Hearers*

MATTHEW 7:(15-20) 21-29

A Satisfied Customer

The famous Danish theologian Soren Kierkegaard once wrote a vivid parable concerning the danger of becoming just a satisfied customer with religion, an occupation so absorbing that it left no inclination to do anything about it.

He imagined that near the cross of Christ had stood a man who beheld the terrible scene, and then became a professor of what he saw. He explained it all.

Later he witnessed the persecution and imprisonment and cruel beating of the apostles and became professor of what he had witnessed.

He studied the drama of the cross, but he was never crucified with Christ in his own life. He studied apostolic history, but he did not live apostolically.

He was an observer and a talker *about* Christianity, but not a doer.

Third Sunday After Pentecost   *Follow Me*

MATTHEW 9:9-13

The Leap of Faith

Remember the last time you went to a circus and saw an acrobat swinging on a trapeze bar high above the crowd? Remember that one breath-taking moment when the performer let go of the bar—hung for one breathless moment in midair—and then grasped the next bar swinging towards him?

That's what people have paid thousands of dollars over the years to see—not a man hanging on a bar, but for that one split second when he lets go and reaches out for the next bar.

Christ says: "Follow Me."

What are you hanging on to right now which you need to let go of? What crippling anxiety, deadening routine, self-centered pastime? Christ calls out to you to be His disciple, in faith. He bids: "Follow Me."

Are you willing to make that reach?

—Adapted from Keith Miller, quoting Paul Tournier in
The Becomers, Word Books, pp. 162—163

Fourth Sunday After Pentecost   *Laborers for the Harvest*

MATTHEW 9:35—10:8

Going—Not Just Listening

A wild goose was brought down by a hunter's lucky shot one day. But only his one wing was wounded, and he finally landed in a barnyard. The domestic ducks, geese, and chickens were quite startled by this sudden visitor from outer space, but they soon sidled up to him and asked him to describe what it was like to fly.

He extolled the glories of flight, remarking how thrilling it was to soar out in the wild blue yonder. "Why, this barn down here looks like it's only an inch high," he said, "and you are all but specks seen from such a distance." And the domestic fowl were quite impressed by his little speech and some time later asked him again to describe the glories of flight.

And it got to be quite a weekly occasion, while the goose's wing was healing, for him to get up in front of the others and talk. They even provided a little box to stand on so they could see him better.

But do you know what happened? While the domestic fowl very much enjoyed hearing *about* the glories of flight, they never tried to fly themselves. And the wild goose, well, even though his wing healed, he just continued to talk about flying—but never flew again.

Christ calls laborers into His harvest. We can talk about it—or we can soar into His service.

—Adapted from a story of Soren Kierkegaard

Fifth Sunday After Pentecost   *God's Protection*

MATTHEW 10:24-33

"Fear Not!"

A young pastor arrived at a conference and commented on how he had narrowly averted a tragic accident. "Isn't that a tremendous demonstration of the way God watched over me?" he asked.

Another pastor said: "Yes, it is a demonstration of God's protective powers. But by coincidence I had an even greater demonstration of God's protective presence in my life this morning. On the way to the conference *nothing* happened!"

—Edmund A. Puseman, *Loyalty Christ and Country,* April 1978

Sixth Sunday After Pentecost   *Sacrificing Self*

MATTHEW 10:34-42

Christ's Help When Needed

Christ calls us to take up our cross and follow Him, and to lose our life for His sake.

Corrie ten Boom recalls struggling with this call as a child, feeling she could never be a martyr for Christ. She confided her fear to her father.

He responded by asking her when he gave her the money for a train ticket for a trip from Haarlem to Amsterdam. Was it three weeks before the trip?

She replied "No"—that he gave her the money for the ticket just before they got on the train.

And he concluded: "That is right. And so it is with God's strength. Our wise Father in heaven knows when you are going to need things too. Today you do not need the strength to be a martyr; but as soon as you are called upon for the honor of facing death for Jesus, He will supply the strength you need—just in time."

—Corrie ten Boom, *Tramp for the Lord,* Pillar Books, p. 117

Seventh Sunday After Pentecost   *I Give Rest*

MATTHEW 11:25-30

A Modern Psalm

> The Lord is my Pacesetter,
>   I shall not rush,
> He makes me stop and rest for quiet intervals.
> He provides me with images of stillness,
>   which restore my serenity.
> He leads me in ways of efficiency through
>   calmness of mind, and His guidance is peace.
> Even though I have a great many things to
>   accomplish each day.
> I will not fret, for His presence is here,
> His timelessness, His all importance will
>   keep me in balance.

He prepares refreshment and renewal in the
　　　midst of my activity,
By anointing my mind with His oils
　　　of tranquility.
My cup of joyous energy overflows.
Surely, harmony and effectiveness shall be
　　　the fruits of my hours,
For I shall walk in the peace of my Lord,
　　　and dwell in His house forever.—Toki Miyashina

Eighth Sunday After Pentecost　　　　　　*The Good Soil*

MATTHEW 13:1-9(18-23)

No Excuse Sundays

To make it possible for everyone to attend church once a month, we are going to have a special "No excuse Sunday" and to insure its success, we offer the following "lures."

1. Cots will be placed in the foyer for those who say: "Sunday is my day to sleep in."

2. There will be a special section with lounge chairs for those who feel that our pews are too hard.

3. Murine will be available for those with tired eyes from watching TV too late on Saturday night.

4. We will have steel helmets for those who think: "The roof will cave in if I ever go to church."

5. Blankets will be furnished for those who think the church is too cold and fans for those who think it is too hot.

6. Score cards will be available for those who wish to list the number of hypocrites present.

7. Relatives and friends will be present for those who like to go visiting on Sunday.

8. There will be TV dinners for those who can't go to church and cook dinner also.

9. We will distribute buttons stating "Stamp Out Collection Envelopes" for those who feel that the church is always asking for money.

10. One section of the church will be devoted to trees and grass for those who like to seek God in nature.

11. A doctor and nurse will be in attendance for those who usually plan to be sick on Sunday.

12. Last but not least, the sanctuary will be decorated with both Christmas poinsettias and Easter lilies for those who have never seen church without them.

　　　　　　　　—*Bulletin,* Roman Catholic Church, Boyne Falls, MI, September 1977

Ninth Sunday After Pentecost　　*God's Judgment on the Age*

MATTHEW 13:24-30(36-43)

The Age—or *You?*

Alvin N. Rogness has noted that if God should find that the scientific ingenuity of our civilization is deflecting us from our real purpose on earth—to live with God and to grow like

God—He may well allow this civilization to perish. A civilization should be judged by what it does for mankind.

"If you were to hear that your boy had been run down while riding his bicycle, you most assuredly would not ask, 'What happened to the bicycle?' Then why should you always be deceived into asking, 'What is going to happen to the age?' when it is not the age, but you, that is important. If, like a defective bicycle, this is a defective age, then perhaps it is a different age or civilization we need, if we are to be saved in the deeper sense!"

—Alvin N. Rogness, *The Age and You*, Augsburg, p. 4

Tenth Sunday After Pentecost   *Judgment*

MATTHEW 13:44-52

Death's Imminence

There was a man who was always afraid that Death would suddenly overtake him and find him unprepared. So he made a bargain with the Grim Reaper that Death would give him clear, repeated notices before he would come.

One day, however, unannounced and altogether unexpectedly, the Destroyer appeared to demand the life of his amazed, trembling victim.

"How could you break your pledge?" the man protested bitterly. "You sent me no warnings."

Slowly the skeletal figure replied: "But how about your failing eyesight, your dimmed sense of hearing, your gray and falling hair, your lost teeth, your furrowed face, your bent body, your dwindling powers, your weakened memory? Were these not unmistakable warnings?"

—Walter A. Maier, *Jesus Christ, Our Hope*, Concordia, p. 204

Eleventh Sunday After Pentecost   *Miracles*

MATTHEW 14:13-21

We are so accustomed to find that grain grows out of the earth annually, and we are so blinded by this that we pay no attention to it; for what we daily see and hear we do not consider a miracle. And yet it is as great a miracle . . . as Christ's feeding the multitude with seven loaves.

—Martin Luther, *What Luther Says*, Ewald Plass, Concordia, 1959, II, 2994

Twelfth Sunday After Pentecost   *Miracles*

MATTHEW 14:22-33

Just Be Sincere

In her book *Children and the Bible* Ethel L. Smither suggests that adults not emphasize the miraculous "at the possible expense of the older child's faith in the reality of Jesus." She recalls an incident which demonstrates the mind of a young child at work upon events beyond his ability to manage.

"Billy, I like your red boots," she told a three-year-old. He smiled and replied: "These are Jesus' boots . . . He lent them to me. He walks on the water with them."

24

Smither concludes, as a result of the child's fantasy, that the religious value of this New Testament story is doubtful for him, and it should have been reserved for later years.

She also concludes that "the miracles should not be used to prove that Jesus was the Son of God. For one reason, there are too many accounts of miracles in the Bible that Jesus did not perform. His own attitude towards His mighty acts of goodness should guide adults also."

—Ethel L. Smither, *Children and the Bible*, Abingdon, p. 42

Thirteenth Sunday After Pentecost — *A Great Faith*

MATTHEW 15:21-28

His Hand Clasping Mine

A minister tells of a woman, a happy and efficient wife of a fellow pastor, who was experiencing her full share of life's sunshine and shade, but with no real darkness falling her way. And then, suddenly, without warning, her husband died of a heart attack, leaving her terribly alone and afraid; afraid of her own decisions, afraid of the present, afraid of the future.

When the minister visited his colleague's wife, he related how she was in the vicelike grip of fear—so tyrannized that most of her time was spent in bed. She was so terrified that she became bedridden.

When the minister saw her two years later, he was pleasantly surprised to find a poised, serene woman, working as a receptionist in an insurance office. When the pastor asked her to explain her amazing recovery, the woman replied, "The work helped, of course, but I couldn't work at all until I faced my fear and saw that it was basically a selfish rebellion against God and what I thought was God's will. When I saw that, I began to pray that God would forgive my selfishness. And as I prayed, I became aware of God's hand reaching down to me, and I somehow began to reach up in faith until I finally clasped that hand. And then to my amazement, I found His hand clasping mine; and I knew that He really cared and that He would help me as long as I held His hand in faith."

Fourteenth Sunday After Pentecost — *Confession*

MATTHEW 16:13-20

Living the Christ-Life

Peter's confession of faith was clear and bold. Is ours always so?

A missionary in China once spoke to a group of people in a town far in the interior. He was the first one to tell them the story of Jesus, and when he had talked a while, someone said: "Oh, yes, we knew Him; He used to live here."

The missionary was somewhat surprised, and said: "Oh, no, He lived centuries ago in another land." But the native still insisted that he had seen Jesus, saying: "Not so, He lived in this village, and we knew Him."

And then the crowd led the missionary to the village cemetery and showed him the grave of a medical missionary who had lived, served, healed, and died in that community.

Years from now when you are dead and gone, and someone else is hearing the story of Jesus for the first time, could that person make this same mistake about you?

"Oh, yes, we knew Him. He used to live here."

Fifteenth Sunday After Pentecost   *Denying One's Self*

MATTHEW 16:21-26

A new "I"

It is said that St. Augustine, accosted on the street by a former mistress shortly after his conversion, turned and walked in the opposite direction.

Surprised, the woman cried out, "Augustine, it is I."

But Augustine, proceeding on his way, cried back to her, "Yes, but it is not I."

C. S. Lewis describes Christ's call to self-denial. "Christ says, 'Give me *all.* I don't want so much of your money and so much of your work—I want *you.* I have not come to torment your natural self, but to kill it. No half-measures are any good. I don't want to cut off a branch here and a branch there, I want to have the whole tree down. I don't want to drill the tooth, or crown it, or stop it, but to have it out. Hand over the whole natural self . . . I will give you a new self instead. In fact I will give you myself, my own will shall become yours.'"

—C.S. Lewis, *Beyond Personality,* Macmillan, p. 40

Sixteenth Sunday After Pentecost   *Forgiveness*

MATTHEW 18:15-20

Feeling Other's Sins as Our Own

Intercession means no more than to bring our brother into the presence of God, to see him under the Cross of Jesus as a poor human being and sinner in need of grace. Then everything in him that repels us falls away; we see him in all his destitution and need. His need and his sin become so heavy and oppressive that we feel them as our own, and we can do nothing else but pray: Lord, do Thou, Thou alone, deal with him according to Thy severity and Thy goodness. To make intercession means to grant our brother the same right that we have received, namely, to stand before Christ and share in his mercy.

—Dietrich Bonhoeffer, *Life Together,* Harper & Row, p. 86

Seventeenth Sunday After Pentecost   *Forgiveness*

MATTHEW 18:21-35

Is It Always Possible?

In *Tramp for the Lord* Corrie ten Boom tells how after the war she met a guard who had been her captor in the Ravensbruck concentration camp where her sister had died. He came forward after she addressed a church gathering, and (though he did not recognize her) said he had been a guard at Ravensbruck, and reached out his hand to her, asking her for forgiveness.

Corrie recalls how she hesitated briefly, remembering how cruel he had been to her, her sister, and so many others. Then, recalling our Lord's words that we are to forgive or we cannot be forgiven, and yet feeling unable to lift her hand towards him, she prayed silently: "Jesus help me! . . . I can lift my hand. I can do that much. You supply the feeling."

And suddenly, she says, she could feel God's power coursing through her hand and out to the former guard.

"I forgive you, brother!" she cried, with all her heart. She says she has never known God's love so powerfully as she did then (pp. 53—55).

Eighteenth Sunday After Pentecost — *Let God Be God*

MATTHEW 20:1-16

Making Deals with God?

An eighteen-year-old girl killed herself on New Year's Day. She left a note describing an agreement she had made "with God, or fate, or something," the year before.

"I agreed that if something did not happen in the year to make life worth living, I'd quit living. That wasn't asking too much, was it?"

Like the workers in the vineyard, does God have to answer to us, or do we answer to God?

Nineteenth Sunday After Pentecost — *Head Knowledge/ Heart Knowledge*

MATTHEW 21:28-32

Knowing by Heart

A little boy was watching a sculptor at work. For weeks this sculptor kept chipping away at a big block of marble. After a few weeks he had created a beautiful marble lion. The little boy was amazed and said: "Mister, how did you know there was a lion in that rock?" (Thomas Hora, *Existential Metaphychiatry,* Seabury Press, 1977).

Henri J. M. Nouwen says the sculptor's secret is to know "by heart" what is in the marble—be it an angel, a demon, or God. The great question is "What do you know by heart?"

He concludes: "Whether the knowledge of the mind leads to God or to the demon depends on the heart. When the Word of God remains a subject of analysis and discussion and does not descend into the heart, it can easily become an instrument of destruction instead of a guide to love. Spiritual formation asks for the ongoing discipline to descend from the mind into the heart so that real knowledge can be found."

—Henri J. M. Nouwen, "What Do You Know by Heart?" *Sojourners,* August 1977

Twentieth Sunday After Pentecost — *Rejection*

MATTHEW 21:33-43

Denying God

"The whole conception of God is a conception derived from the ancient Oriental despotisms. It is a conception quite unworthy of free man. . . . A good world needs knowledge, kindliness, and courage; it does not need a regretful hankering after the past or a fettering of the free intelligence by the words uttered long ago by ignorant men" (Bertrand Russell, 1872—1970).

"As for religion, I am quite devoid of it. The act of worship, as carried on by Christians, seems to me to be debasing rather than ennobling. It involves groveling before a Being, who, if He really exists, deserves to be denounced instead of respected" (Henry Louis Mencken, 1880—1956).

"I want to be able to walk down any street in America and not see a cross or a sign of religion. I won't stop till the Pope—or whoever the highest religious authority is—says that atheists have a right to breathe in this world." (Madalyn Murray O'Hair, 1919—   ).

—Modern Atheists/Agnostics of the Western World,
in David Wallechinsky and Irving Wallace,
The People's Almanac, Doubleday and Co., Inc., pp. 1294—5.

Twenty-First Sunday After Pentecost   *Christ's Wedding Feast*

MATTHEW 22:1-10(11-14)

All Are Invited

On the CBS feature "Newsbreak," Charles Osgood commented on the efforts of a religion editor of one of the Cleveland papers who was conducting an ongoing experiment. Each Sunday this editor would anonymously visit one of the churches in the Cleveland area and give his evaluation of the service he attended.

Following the lead of people who assign stars to restaurants, this man judged the service in four categories—preaching, music, format and fellowship—attributing from one to three stars to each category.

After attending more than twenty-two such various services, he had given the top number of twelve stars to only two congregations. One was a black congregation and the other a Pentecostal store-front situation. In his commentary he was quoted as saying that the loneliest hour of the week may be reserved for a visitor entering a Christian church to join in worship and fellowship. He particularly criticized the "coffee hour" which followed the service and which usually left him standing by himself sipping his coffee while the members chatted with their friends ("Inside Immanuel," newsletter of Immanuel Lutheran Church, Danville, CA, September 1978).

Christ invites all people to His banquet table. But do *we* welcome them?

Twenty-Second Sunday After Pentecost   *God and Caesar*

MATTHEW 22:15-21

The Nation's Need for God

During the Civil War a man spent three weeks visiting Abraham Lincoln in the White House. The night after the Battle of Bull Run he was not able to sleep and as dawn neared and he was walking through the halls, he heard a voice coming from the President's room. As he looked into the room, he saw Abraham Lincoln kneeling before his Bible in prayer. And he heard Lincoln saying, with the deepest sorrow: "O Thou God, that heard Solomon in the night when he prayed and cried for wisdom, hear me! I cannot lead this people, I cannot guide the affairs of this nation without Thy help. I am poor and weak and sinful. O God, Thou didst hear Solomon when he cried for wisdom—hear me and save this nation."

Twenty-Third Sunday After Pentecost

Loving God/
Loving Others

MATTHEW 22:34-40(41-46)

An Unbeatable Combination

Corrie ten Boom once described a tall black man in Africa named Thomas who lived in a round hut with his large family as "a man who loved the Lord and loved people—an unbeatable combination" (*Tramp for the Lord,* p. 75).

That is quite a combination, isn't it?

Thomas P. Malone once observed that most emotional problems can be summed up in the kind of behavior where a person walks around screaming, "For God's sake, love me."

"On the other hand, healthy people are those who walk around looking for someone to love. And, if you see changes in the people who were screaming, 'Love me, love me,' it's when they realize that if they give up this screaming and go to the other business of loving another human, they can get the love they've been screaming for all their lives. It's hard to learn, but it's good when you learn it" (Thomas P. Malone, in *Guideposts,* quoted in *Your Church,* July-August 1975, p. 6).

How tragic when it can be said of us, as Scobie's wife said of him in Graham Greene's *The Heart of the Matter:* "It is certain that he loved God, but it is also certain that he loved no one else."

Last Sunday After Pentecost
(Christ the King)

Readiness

MATTHEW 25:1-13

You've Given Me Time

"You've given me time." These were the telling words which the author of "The Gathering" put into the mouth of the father (played by Ed Asner) in the pre-Christmas special on TV. The father, talking with his doctor, had just discovered how few days he still had to live. Then how could he say, "You've given me time"? Suddenly what counted for the father was not the amount of minutes, but the way they would be used. Those who watched "The Gathering" found the father using the limited time to heal, mend, reconcile family relationships, which prior to that new reality had been postponed and avoided. Hence the reality of the words "You've given me time."

The Scriptures consider time a sign of grace, for only where we have time do we have *opportunity*—a chance to do the will of God, those things which are important, which count. . . .

You and I need to realize the precious gift God has given us: *time.* Let's not waste it. Let's use it to celebrate the graciousness of God and thankfully shout, "Thanks, God, You've given me time!"

—Adapted from Paul Meyer, *Trinity Trumpet,*
Trinity Lutheran Church, Walnut Creek, CA, January 1978

Reformation Day

Reformation

JOHN 8:31-36

The Three Reformers

You're acquainted with them of course—the three reformers? First there is God. He's the greatest Reformer of all. Through the death and resurrection of Jesus Christ, God has begun the cosmic reformation, making all things beautiful and new. And when the Savior returns in glory, God will once again pronounce the approving word over His restored and recreated world: "Very good!"

Then there was Martin Luther, the man whose exploits we celebrate during these Reformation days. What a giant he was as under God he brought an errant and straying church back to her moorings, stubbornly and bravely insisting that Christ alone redeems us to God.

And who's the third reformer? Why you, of course. You're both reformed and reformer. Your baptism day was your great Reformation Day. That's when God completely reformed, reshaped, revamped you, made you to look and live and love like Christ His Son. And it's that Christ-like love which is your power to carry on your daily reformation—first of yourself and then of your world. Behold how the darkness disappears as God's living lights shine.

—Herbert Hohenstein, *Unity News,*
Unity Lutheran Church, Bel Nor, MO, Oct. 27, 1977

Index of Scripture Texts

Index of Topics

Gospel Lessons, Series B

by
Gerhard Aho
George Bass
Daniel Benuska
Erwin J. Kolb
Bruce Lieske

Contributors

First Sunday in Advent Through the Fourth Sunday After Epiphany—Rev. Bruce J. Lieske.

Fifth Sunday After Epiphany Through the Monday of Holy Week—Rev. Daniel A. Benuska.

Tuesday of Holy Week Through the Day of Pentecost—Dr. Gerhard Aho.

Holy Trinity (First Sunday After Pentecost) Through the Fourteenth Sunday After Pentecost—Dr. Erwin J. Kolb.

Fifteenth Sunday After Pentecost Through the Last Sunday of the Church Year—Dr. George M. Bass.

Sources—Series B

World Aflame, Billy Graham, Billy Graham Evangelistic Assoc., 1965

Our Daily Bread, June-August 1980, Radio Bible Class

The People's Almanac, Doubleday & Company, 1975

Ministry, July 1980

For Men Only, J. Allan Petersen, Tyndale, 1977

The Lutheran Witness, July 1980

The Psychology of Religion, Walter Houston Clark, Macmillan Co., New York, 1967

The Marriage Encounter, Fr. Chuck Gallagher, Doubleday & Co., Inc., Garden City, NY, 1975

Pulpit Resource, Vol. 8, No. 3, July-August-September 1980

In Season, "True Greatness," Robert Hausman, Cathedral Publishers, Royal Oak, MI, November 4, 1979

A Treasury of Inspirational Illustrations, Earl C. Willer, Baker Book House, Grand Rapids, MI, © 1975

The Cross in Agony and Ecstasy, Herbert F. Lindemann, Concordia, 1973

Living Lenten Portraits, Richard Andersen, Concordia, 1975

Were You There? Erich H. Heintzen, Concordia, 1958

King Forever, James S. Stewart, Abingdon, Nashville, 1975

The Twentieth Century Pulpit, Fulton J. Sheen, Abingdon, Nashville, 1978

Christ and the Meaning of Life, Helmut Thielicke, Baker, Grand Rapids, MI 1975

The Gospel for Kids, Series B, Eldon Weisheit, Concordia, 1978

Hastings Illustrations, Robert J. Hastings, Broadman, Nashville, 1971

Illustrations for Preaching, Benjamin P. Browne, Broadman, Nashville, 1977

Life Sentence, Charles Colson, Chosen Books, 1979, pp. 105—6

Liberty, "The Blue Laws of New England," January-February 1963, pp. 18—19

Faith at Work, "The Church Needs Repatterning," August 1973

Time, August 4, 1980, p. 26 and p. 54

American Bible Society Tract, *"I hope so, I think so, Yes, I know so!"* C. A. Van Andel

Francis Scott Key: Life and Times, Edward S. Delaplaine, as quoted in "The Star Spangled Banner," *Decision,* July 1980

Portals of Prayer, Herman Gockel, July 18, 1980

Born Again, Charles Colson

The Holy Spirit, Billy Graham

The Supreme Possession, G. Ray Jordan, Abingdon-Cokesbury, NY 1945

Reaching Out: The Three Movements of Spiritual Life, Henri J. M. Nouwen, Doubleday, New York, 1975, p. 84

The Concordia Pulpit, Concordia Publishing House, 1972

American Bible Society Record, June-July 1980

The Star Thrower, Loren Eiseley

First Sunday in Advent
Second Coming of Christ

MARK 13:33-37

Wake Up—Your House Is on Fire!

"Mr. Average Man is comfortable in his complacency and as unconcerned as a silverfish ensconced in a carton of discarded magazines on world affairs. Man is not asking any questions, because his social benefits from the government give him a false security. This is his trouble and his tragedy. Modern man has become a spectator of world events, observing on his television screen without becoming involved. He watches the ominous events of our times pass before his eyes, while he sips his beer in a comfortable chair. He does not seem to realize what is happening to him. He does not understand that his world is on fire and that he is about to be burned with it."

—Billy Graham, *World Aflame,* The Billy Graham Evangelistic Association, 1965

Second Sunday in Advent
Baptism of the Holy Spirit

MARK 1:1-8

Thirsty for God

Water is essential to human life. Medical authorities tell us that the body needs about 3 quarts a day to operate efficiently. The blood, which is 90 percent H_2O, carries nutrients to the cells. As a cooling agent, water regulates our temperature through perspiration. And without its lubricating properties, our joints and muscles would grind and creak like unused parts of some old rusty machinery. That drink of cool, clear water does more than quench your thirst. It provides your body with the life-giving liquid it must have!

Jesus likened the Holy Spirit to living water (John 4:10; 7:37-39; cf. also 1 Cor. 12:13b). He baptizes us with the Holy Spirit. The new born-again man needs the cleansing, refreshing, life-giving water of the Holy Spirit just as the natural body needs H_2O to sustain it.

—Adapted from *Our Daily Bread,* June-August 1980, Radio Bible Class

Third Sunday in Advent
Bearing Witness to Jesus

JOHN 1:6-8, 19-28

One Thing Thou Lackest!

Once when George Whitefield, powerful preacher of repentance, had been the guest in a wealthy family, he saw to his dismay that the Son of God had no abiding place in that home. Before he left, he took a diamond ring and scratched on the window pane of his room, "One thing thou lackest!" Afterward, the wife of his host passed through the room Whitefield had occupied. She paused suddenly before the window to read, "One thing thou lackest!" These four words pierced her heart. She called her husband, and her daughters. They, too, were struck by the warning, "One thing thou lackest!" Then came the realization that with their money, the beauty and comfort of their home, they were without Jesus. Whitefield's unusual witness to Jesus helped to bring that whole family to repentance and faith.

—Source unknown

Fourth Sunday in Advent   *Honoring the Savior*

LUKE 1:26-38

Accept What the Savior Did for You

Once upon a time there was a perfect kingdom. Nothing ever went wrong because the penalty for wrongdoing was death. But one day somebody *did* break a law. Let us suppose that person was you. You are placed on death row, awaiting execution. You hear the steps of the guards. They are coming for you. They go past you. Somebody else is taken. The death hood is placed over that person, and he is marched out into the courtyard. Shots ring out, and the man dies. Then you hear a grief-stricken cry from the king. He has just read a note which says: "I have died for this person. Forgive him, release him." The king's very own son has died for you! Then the guards appear at your cell and tell you that you are free to go.

What is your response? "No thanks, king, I really don't deserve to be in jail anyway—some day I'm going to dig my way out of here with a spoon."

—Source unknown

The Nativity of Our Lord (1)   *Praising God*

LUKE 2:1-20

Praise God Where You Are

Suppose a close member of your family went to law school and became a successful lawyer. One day he went into politics and was elected to the House of Representatives. He distinguished himself with wise, honest leadership. Then he decided to run for president, and was elected. Imagine yourself in Washington, D.C., on a crisp, cold day in January. That member of your family has just finished his inaugural address as President of the United States. You rise to your feet, and what do you do? If you are little brother, you clap your hands louder than anybody else. If you are the big sister, you put your arms around your brother and hug him. If you are dad, you shake your son's hand and say "Good speech, son." And if you are mom, you just smile through your tears. All of these are different expressions of *praise*—acknowledging the greatness of someone you love.

—Bruce J. Lieske

The Nativity of Our Lord (2)   *Grace*

JOHN 1:1-14

Grace upon Grace

Every family has its unique Christmas traditions. In our home we had the "brownies," mythical elves who were the forerunners of Santa. They made their presence known in our household about a week before Christmas. My brother and I carefully hung our stockings on the mantle and hoped each morning that the "brownies" would leave a small toy, a package of gum, or some other goody. But we were solemnly warned that if our behavior was bad during the day the "brownies" would not hesitate to put a lump of coal in our stocking.

I never believed this could happen to me. Perhaps somebody else would get the coal, but not me. Then it happened. In my memory is a photographic image of myself, with tear-stained face, showing my mother the horrid piece of coal. My mother calmly explained that I had received what I deserved. As Christmas grew nearer my six-year-old mind began to dwell on the words of that old familiar song "Santa Claus Is Coming to Town." Would disaster strike again? The words *did* say "You'd better watch out, you'd better watch out, you'd better not cry, you'd better not pout, . . . he's making a list, checking it twice, going to find out who's naughty and who's nice."

What joy I experienced that Christmas, unwrapping my presents and discovering in my childlike way that my parents gave me presents not because I deserved them, but because they loved me.

—Bruce J. Lieske

The First Sunday After Christmas
The Infinite Worth of Jesus

LUKE 2:25-38

The Precious Child

Years ago someone was going door to door soliciting contributions for a Christian orphanage. The solicitor approached one exasperated housewife and asked, "Would you like to give a donation to such and such orphanage?" He was surprised when the housewife said, "Yes, just a minute and I'll get them—they are ages two and three."

Christian parents may have moments of exasperation with their children, but nevertheless they recognize their children as precious gifts of God. God gave his Son, Jesus, to us. And He did it by giving Him as a child. Simeon and Anna recognized that the baby Jesus was precious. Do you?

—Adapted from an unknown source

The Second Sunday After Christmas
Growth in Sanctification

JOHN 1:1-18

Who Gets the Help?

In June 1972 Hurricane Agnes struck the eastern United States, dumping its heaviest rainfall on northeastern Pennsylvania. The Susquehanna River overflowed its dikes at Wilkes-Barre. 200,000 people were in need of rescue and relief. Looting followed the destruction of the business districts of Wilkes-Barre and Kingston and even private homes became prey for looters. Flood victims, dazed by the destruction of their property, feared the loss of what remained.

Lutheran churches in the area quickly organized a relief and rescue operation, with its headquarters at St. Matthew Lutheran Church, Wilkes-Barre. Food, blankets, and small household items were donated by Lutherans from all over Pennsylvania. Pastors, wearing blue jeans, boots and clerical collars walked the streets offering help. Some refused help. But most people trusted the pastors and Christian volunteers. They gladly received them into their damaged homes. Those Christians then shoveled out the mud, washed down the walls, and helped make repairs.

Jesus would enter the door of every human heart. *Whoever receives Him*—trusting Him as Savior—is born again of God. And that is the person who gets the help, the power, to become God-like!

—*The People's Almanac*, Doubleday and Company, 1975

The Epiphany of Our Lord   *Financial Stewardship*

MATTHEW 2:1-12

What Is It Worth to You?

People show how much they value something by means of money. A community that does not highly value education will pay its teachers low salaries. Many people don't hesitate to pay $8 for 4/5 of a quart of whiskey ($40 per gallon if you want to compare it to the cost of gasoline). J. T. Molloy, author of the best-selling book *Dress for Success* (for men), discovered that the *value* of a man's clothing is important in determining his credibility and acceptance. People who are well dressed receive preferential treatment in almost all social and business encounters.

The word "worship" derives from the old English word "worth-ship." An act of worship is any act whereby we give *value* to God. The Wise Men laid gold, frankincense, and myrrh at the feet of Jesus, thereby showing that He had *value* for them. How highly do *you* value Jesus and His church? How much are you paying your pastor, the teachers in your parochial school, your organist?

—Material taken from *Ministry,* July 1980

The Baptism of Our Lord   *Repentance*
First Sunday After the Epiphany

MARK 1:4-11

Repent and Be Saved

In 1963 the scientific research station ARLIS II (Arctic Research Laboratory Ice Station) was located close to the North Pole, drifting in a jumble of sea ice over 1,000 miles from its resupply station at Pt. Barrow, Alaska. A dozen or so men manned the station. Food supplies were not critical, but the ARLIS II supply of diesel oil was down to one barrel.

The diesel oil was needed to run a generator that provided electricity for the station. It was especially important that the radio navigation beacon have power because without it the resupply plane—long delayed—would be unable to find the station in the vast polar wastes. In mid-September, with the long polar night just beginning, the ski-equipped DC-3 took off. But while the plane was enroute, an ionospheric storm blacked out all radio communication between it and ARLIS II. The plane continued to fly in the general direction of the station, urgently radioing in the blind, "Turn on your beacon." Radioman Gary Sides at ARLIS II heard only static on his radio. Finally he lost hope and turned off his radio. He didn't know that the plane was close by and was about to turn around and go back to Pt. Barrow.

For some unknown reason, the radioman *turned back* to his radio, flicked the switch to "on" and heard the pilot say " . . . beacon on." Instantly he realized what had happened. He quickly switched on the navigation beacon. The plane landed safely within the hour and the men were saved. If the radioman had not "repented" and turned back to his radio, the men would all have perished.

—Bruce J. Lieske

Second Sunday After the Epiphany   *Obedience to Christ*

JOHN 1:43-51

Obedience Blessed by God

"The renowned preacher Donald Grey Barnhouse told of a missionary in Africa whose little son was playing in the yard. Suddenly he heard his father's voice. 'Philip! Obey me instantly! Drop to the ground!' The boy did what he was told without any question. 'Now crawl toward me as fast as you can.' Again the boy obeyed. 'Now stand up and run to me!' The lad followed instructions and ended in his father's arms. Only then did he look back at the tree where he had been playing. *Hanging from a limb was a 15-foot snake!* Suppose the boy had paused to ask why, or in a whining tone had inquired, 'Do I have to do that right now?' He would have been killed by that deadly reptile."

Jesus told Philip the Apostle, "Follow me." He did. The result was the conversion of Nathanael.

—Our Daily Bread, June-August 1980, Radio Bible Class

Third Sunday After the Epiphany *Repentance*

MARK 1:14-20

We Need the Call to Repentance

"Nature has generously equipped most animals with a fear of things that could be harmful to them, but did not protect the frog quite so well. If a frog is placed in a pan of warm water under which the heat is being increased very gradually, he will typically show no inclination to escape. As the temperature continues to intensify, the frog remains oblivious to his danger; he could easily hop his way to safety, but he is apparently thinking about something else. He will just sit there, contentedly peering over the edge of the pan while the steam curls ominously around his nostrils. Eventually the boiling frog will pass on to his reward, having succumbed to a misfortune he could easily have avoided.

"Human beings have some of the same perceptual inadequacies as their little green friends. We quickly become excited about *sudden* dangers that confront us. However, if a threatening problem arises very slowly, perhaps over a decade or two, we often allow ourselves to 'boil' in happy ignorance."

Fourth Sunday After the Epiphany *Witchcraft/Occult*

MARK 1:21-28

Victory over Demons in the Name of Jesus

"They sat in a circle, holding hands. The room was dark, except for the dim light cast by a flickering candle in the center of the ring. An aroma of incense floated through the air as Madame Zerkee chanted, 'The one the candle flame points to will be the one through whom the spirit will speak.'

Suddenly a young mother of two screamed and fell off her chair. As she lay unconscious on the floor, a voice not her own began speaking to the group.

Meanwhile in another city, the chauffeur driving three members of a top money-making rock group, asked what its name stood for.

'It means we're in Satanic service,' replied one of the young masked millionaires, as their car sped toward a concert date and a waiting audience of thousands of impressionable teenagers . . .

The Reverend T. W. Polster, recognized church authority on the occult, of Our Savior Lutheran Church of San Jose, California, states, 'Demons are on the increase. Since 1963 we've had an influx of demons empowered to do strange things that they couldn't do before.'

. . . Demons were real in Bible times and they are real today. They separate us from God. While Christians continue to buy and use 'harmless' ouija boards and rock records, memorize character traits of their sun signs, and thank their 'lucky stars' instead of God, demons are making inroads."

But in the name of Jesus we have authority over Satan and his hosts! And as our Lord Jesus has promised, "Nothing shall hurt you" (Luke 10:19).

—The Lutheran Witness, July 1980

Fifth Sunday After the Epiphany   *Suffering/Sickness*

MARK 1:29-39

Who Plays You?

There's the story of a small town in New Mexico that decided to have an auction to raise money for a community center. The townsfolk looked through closets and drawers, investigated their attics and garages, collected trinkets, odds and ends of furniture, and white elephants and brought them to the auction center. One by one the auctioneer would hold them up for a bid, and so they were sold. The last item to be auctioned off was an old violin. It was dusty and dirty and covered with spatterings of paint. It obviously had lain in the back of someone's garage unused for years. Finally the auctioneer held it up. "What am I bid," he called out. There was only silence. "Come on," he persisted, "say something." Finally someone yelled out, "Fifty cents," and everybody laughed. Then from the back of the group an old man, whom no one knew, came to the front and asked to see the violin. He took it into his arms and began to play it. Its beautiful sound filled the room and touched everyone's heart. When he finished, he handed the violin back to the auctioneer and walked away. "What am I bid," the auctioneer called out again. "$200! $300! $400!" and so the bids went on.[1]

You see we're all very much like that old violin. What becomes of us depends on who plays us. And what becomes of our sickness depends on who plays it too. For some, sickness (their own or another's) is only a tragedy without purpose or meaning. But when Christ plays our life, not only our health but our sickness has a different sound to it. Such is the tone of this prayer of Blaise Pascal: "I ask Thee for neither health nor sickness, neither life nor death, but that Thou mayest dispose of my health and sickness for Thy glory, for my salvation, and for the good of the Church, and of Thy saints."[2]

[1] Dan Benuska—retold from a story heard on the radio passing through T or C, New Mexico.
[2] Walter Houston Clark, *The Psychology of Religion* (New York: The Macmillan Company, 1967) pp. 319, 320.

Sixth Sunday After the Epiphany   *Witness*

MARK 1:40-45

Everyone Can Tell

I am told the Church of the Holy Nativity in Bethlehem uses a special kind of incense for its worship services. As worshipers leave the church and mingle with people in the crowded streets, heads turn. Everyone can tell where they've been. The sweet incense of Nativity clings to their clothing and hangs all about them. In spite of themselves they become walking advertisements for the One they've worshiped. So it was for the leper who was touched and healed by Jesus. Told to be silent, he had to talk about it and share it. The joy of new life with Jesus and the incense of Jesus' compassion was so much a part of his life, he couldn't separate anything he had to say from it. He had to advertise Jesus. It's like that with everyone who's been with Jesus.

—Dan Benuska

Seventh Sunday After the Epiphany   *Service*

MARK 2:1-12

I Have No Hands but Yours!

As I read the story of the healing of the paralytic, I was struck by the sideline figures in the drama. There are the religious leaders. They come only to criticize and judge, to grumble and complain. Unmoved and indifferent to the paralytic's problem, they lift no hand to help him. The crowd, too, gathered tight, standing shoulder to shoulder, will not give an inch.

They too will not move to help him. How different are those four friends of the paralytic. Nothing, neither the thick crowd nor thick roof, will stop them from getting their friend to Jesus, getting him to the place of healing. Their muscles and minds, their hands and hearts show their love and concern. Father Chuck Gallagher tells the story of American soldiers that had fought all day for a small town in Germany. Then, just before nightfall, they captured it. When they marched into the village square, there lying in pieces was a statue of Christ which had been knocked off its pedestal by the artillery bombardment. Over the course of the next several days, they gathered it up and carefully began to put it together. On finally completing the job, they discovered the hands were missing. Nonetheless, they decided to put it back on its pedestal. The next morning a crudely lettered cardboard sign was hanging across the handless arms. It said, "I have no hands but yours."[1]

[1] Fr. Chuck Gallagher, S.J., *The Marriage Encounter* (Garden City, N.Y.: Doubleday and Company, Inc., 1975) p. 19.

—Dan Benuska

Eighth Sunday After the Epiphany *Freedom/Bondage*

MARK 2:18-22

You Can't Please Everyone

One of the most persistent and familiar "yokes of slavery" is being enslaved to what others think of us and expect of us. We live trying to earn everyone else's approval. We are tortured by worry because someone ignored us or didn't smile at us. "What did I do now?" We're disturbed and crushed by a word of censure or criticism. It ruins our day. We become what one psychologist called "Approvaholics." I wonder if it really is possible to please everyone—all the time?

There is a story about a wife who had a husband she felt she could never please. She made up her mind that she was going to do something that would draw approval from him—no matter what it was. Early the next morning, she got up and asked him, "Dear, what would you like for breakfast?" His response was: "two eggs, one fried and one scrambled, toast and coffee." She dutifully hurried to the kitchen and worked hard at making this a memorable breakfast that he would not forget. She set the table with special care, and even picked fresh flowers from the garden to put on the table. When she finished, she called him to breakfast. He shuffled through the door and sat down. She stood beside him with anticipation, waiting for his compliment. A word of approval. Finally he said, "You did it again. You went and scrambled the wrong egg!" (Adapted from a story told in *Clergy Talk,* Tomlinson Publishing Co., Garden Grove, CA) Even Jesus couldn't please everyone. We all have to realize that there are some people we can never please no matter how hard we try. We also have to realize and remember that it's not what others say or don't say about us that determines us, but what God has said about us in Christ Jesus: "You're somebody special, the only one of a kind. I found you, I love you, I redeemed you. You're Mine." That's what the apostle Paul meant when he wrote: "Such is the confidence that we have through Christ toward God," and, "our competence is from God" (2 Cor. 3:4 ff. and the Epistle for this day).

—Dan Benuska

Transfiguration *Point of Reference*
Last Sunday After the Epiphany

MARK 9:2-9

A Rock in Your Pocket

My friend Wayne told me about an interim job he took after graduating from college. It was in a rope-making factory. The factory didn't just make small ropes, ordinary ropes, but huge ropes, the kind of ropes capable of holding a ship in dock.

"What do you know about making ropes?" they asked. He replied, "Not much, but I can learn." "How do you know you can learn?" "Well, I'm a college graduate." So they hired him and sent him into the factory to his own machine. The individual strands would enter the machine on one side and rush out the other end all woven together. It seemed so obvious, so simple. His job was to see to it that the individual strands were fed in properly and then as the single, great diameter rope came out the other side to grab it and put it into place. As Wayne stood before the machine the man next to him said, "Do you got a rock in your pocket?" "What?" Wayne answered. "Do you got a rock in your pocket?" I didn't know what on earth he was talking about, and not wanting to appear dumb, I simply said, "Oh, yeh, oh sure." I would soon know what he meant.

It was simple to feed the rope in, but the rope came out with such force and power that when I grabbed onto it, determined to do it right, it swept me off my feet and lifted me right off the ground into the air. I came down with an embarrassing crash and with all my confidence and bravado and college degree scattered over the floor. I knew then what he meant about a rock in my pocket. Yes, that's the way it is; some things require a rock in your pocket, a point of reference, or else you'll get swept right off your feet, out of control and off base. Jesus knew that. That's why he took Peter and James and John to the mountain top. He knew they needed a rock in their pocket, a point of reference, to view the hard road that lay ahead of Him. Christ's transfiguration is the rock in our Lenten pocket. It's ballast in suffering, a vantage point for what lies ahead for Christ and for us. Nothing can separate us from God's love in Jesus Christ. The victory is His and will be ours too.

—Dan Benuska

Ash Wednesday   *Guilt/Confession*

MATTHEW 6:1-6 (16-18) (19-21)

Uncovering the Cover Up

The couple decided to remodel their home. After securing a home improvement loan, they hired carpenters to raise the ceiling and build in bookcases, masons to put in a fireplace, painters to paint, and then they ran low on money. The young man decided that he'd have to put in the carpeting himself. A trip to the library provided him with the necessary books to tell him how to do it. When he had read them and felt he was ready, he measured and calculated, bought the necessary tools, and ordered the carpet. Early that Saturday morning he started. He cleared out the furniture, carefully laid down the padding, unrolled and stretched out the carpeting, carefully nailing it down. Several exhausting hours later he was finished.

Standing up to admire his work, he reached into his pocket for a cigarette. The pocket was empty. He thought he remembered something slipping out of his pocket. He looked around the newly laid carpet and there several feet from one end he noticed a lump. "Oh, no," he groaned. He walked over to the spot and said, "There's no way I'm going to tear it loose and start over." So he lifted his foot and brought it down hard, squashing it down. Then he put an end table over the spot. "No one will ever know," he thought. Satisfied, he went into the kitchen announcing to his wife, "I'm all finished" and then continued, "Oh, honey, did you see my cigarettes?" "Oh, yes," she replied, "they're right here on the window sill where you left them. And by the way did you see the parakeet?"[1]

It seems someone always pays for the sins we hope to cover up. Lent is a time to uncover our hearts, to admit our sins. Our sins are sins, dark and dirty and destructive, nothing to brag or boast about. So quietly, without fanfare, we gather to confess our sins before God. We come to hear the Word of forgiveness. We come to feel the sign of the cross traced on our forehead. "You are dust and to dust you shall return. But I have covered your nakedness. I have hidden your sins behind My back." Yes, thanks be to God who gives us the victory in Jesus Christ!

¹ Adapted from a story told by Pastor Ted Hartman.

—Dan Benuska

First Sunday in Lent   *Temptation*

MARK 1:12-15

True Optimism in Temptation

The problem of many people who talk about fighting temptation is that they assume we have the reserve and resolve, the will power and strength to do it. They often have an optimistic understanding of the nature of people. Ogden Nash satirically wrote, "I can resist anything except temptation"; and, "The only way to get rid of temptation is to give in to it." There's more truth in his words then we'd like to admit.

La Rochefoucould in *Maxims* (1665) put it this way: "When we resist temptation, it is usually because temptation is weak, not because we are strong."

It's extremely important that we recognize both the strength of our temptations and our limited strength in dealing with them. Only then will we begin to understand all that Christ has done for us. It is not because we have won the battles of life that we are confident but because Christ has. It is not because we are so cock sure of our strength that we face temptation but because we're sure of His presence by us and His power for us.

In the TV movie *Eric,* we watched young Eric's struggle with cancer. There's a touching moment when he stands on the beach of their summer home with his father. "Daddy," he says, "remember how I wanted to swim across the bay with you. We got half way across and I said I couldn't make it. You reached out and held onto me? Well, Daddy, I don't think I can make it now." Eric's father quietly spread his arms around him and said, "I won't let you go down. Put your arms around my neck, and we'll go on together."

—Dan Benuska

Second Sunday in Lent   *Crossbearing*

MARK 8:31-38

Your Cross Is Killing Me!

Throughout the Lenten Season I often get caught up in a whirlwind of movement and activity. I feel like I'm running in a million directions. Usually it's my family that suffers. In the midst of one of those days, I was hurrying out the door when my wife reminded me to tell our youngest daughter good-bye. "Hurry up, hurry up," I clamored, "Dad's got work to do."

Around my neck I was wearing a cross and figure of Christ made from horseshoe nails. As I grabbed Sarah roughly and pulled her up she yelled out. My cross had put a deep scratch in her face. "Dad," she cried with tears in her eyes, "your cross is killing me!" Ironically, even our own crossbearing can be a burden and cross for another. I used to wear a cross around my neck as a kind of calling card for others. Now I wear it for myself. As Henri J. M. Nouwen points out, at best we're all "wounded healers." *(The Wounded Healer* Doubleday and Company, [Garden City, N.Y.: 1972])

—Dan Benuska

Third Sunday in Lent   *Discipline*

JOHN 2:13-22

Broken Legs and Broken Tables

The picture of an angry Jesus, whip in hand, slashing and smashing, driving out the money changers from the Jerusalem temple is shocking and startling to us. We are more accustomed to a mild-mannered, tenderhearted, long-suffering portrait of the good teacher and good shepherd of Nazareth. Love sometimes hurts and can call for stern measures.

God's love is active, not passive. Disciple comes from the word discipline. Discipline can be a proof of caring. Glendon Harris in a sermon, "Discipline: A High Form of Love," tells the story of Montana shepherds who practice an ancient seemingly cruel means of handling that occasional "black sheep" of independent habit who wanders away from the flock. The shepherd deliberately breaks one of the sheep's legs. This is done so the sheep will follow the shepherd after he has nursed it back to health. If not done, the sheep would invariably stray into dangerous places and get killed.[1]

[1] *Pulpit Resource*, Vol. 8, No. 3, July-August-September 1980

—Dan Benuska

Fourth Sunday in Lent   *Redemption*

JOHN 3:14-21

The Rag Picker

As a boy growing up in Cleveland, I remember the "rag picker." In the spring of the year he would walk down the streets behind his pushcart calling out, "Rags, rags, rags!" People would come from their houses with piles of rags and scraps and bits and pieces of cloth in odd shapes and sizes. "What does he do with the rags?" I asked my mother. I could see no use or value in them. "He makes loop rugs," she replied, "beautiful things. He takes those discarded bits and pieces and weaves them together and makes something useful from them."

So it is with Jesus. "All our righteousness is as filthy rags," Paul wrote. "God so loved the world that He gave His only Son, gave Him to pick up the rags of our life. Jesus is able to take the bad parts as well as the good parts of our life, weave them together on the loom of the cross and make something beautiful from them. He lifts them up and says, "See, Father, see how beautiful I have made their rags." Yes, in Jesus, it can be seen clearly that our deeds have been wrought in God!

—Dan Benuska

Fifth Sunday in Lent   *Redemption*

JOHN 12:20-33

The Star Thrower

The way of the cross, this losing of one's life for others is not for Jesus alone. His way of life for us not only brought us life, but is to be our way of life. To use others for one's life is the one way of life. To use one's life for others is another way of life. It is the way of Christ, and eternal life. Loren Eiseley's book, *The Unexpected Universe,* has a chapter entitled "The Star Thrower." Eiseley tells of an incident that happened on a tropical beach. During a certain time, the surf would cast shellfish onto the shore. Professional collectors and sellers greedily descended on the beach, swooping them up to cart them home, to boil them, to clean out the living creatures and sell the shells. On the far end of the beach he watched a lonely figure, stooping, picking up starfish one by one and throwing them back into the sea. "Do you collect?" Eiseley asked him. "Only like this," he said, throwing another into the water. "I collect only for the living. See, one can help them."

In the midst of a world where multitudes callously exploit the dying universe and a dying people for their own benefit, came one solitary figure. Like the star thrower, he moved among the debris of humanity. His mission was one of rescuing, reclaiming, and restoring those who lay helpless, stranded on the shore, tossed up by the storms of life. He gave Himself as a ransom for us and in that self-giving is the key to our freedom and our life. His voice calls us from the cross and echoes in the empty tomb: "Come, follow Me. Lift high the cross. Serve as I have served you. Stoop down and become a star thrower too."

—Adapted from Robert Hausman's Sermon, "True Greatness." *In Season* (Royal Oak, Mich.: Cathedral Publishers, Nov. 4, 1979)

—Dan Benuska

Sunday of the Passion Palm Sunday

Perseverance

MARK 14:1-15—15:47

The Trailblazers

As the early Christians gathered in Jerusalem for Holy Week, they came to relive Jesus' journey to the cross and to remember that they too were called to follow in His footsteps. They were to be His ambassadors and representatives. They knew that following Him took preparation and persistence. They knew the journey to the place of alleluias must first cross the steep slope of Golgotha.

The Trailblazers is the story of the Lewis and Clark Expedition into Louisiana Territory. The two-and-a-half-year journey, begun in the spring of 1803 and ending in the autumn of 1806, would pass through 7,689 miles of dangerous, uncharted wilderness. The journey was not a spur of the moment lark, but took years of preparation. Meriwether Lewis was only a teenager when Thomas Jefferson first proposed the trip. Lewis was trained to detail Indian life, their customs, medicine, diet, and religious practices. Robert Patterson tutored him in celestial navigation. Benjamin Smith Barton, naturalist; Caspar Wistar, anatomist; and Dr. Benjamin Rush, physician; are listed among his teachers. Every Christian disciple and trailblazer has a list of teachers behind him.

Throughout the journey Lewis kept a diary of his findings and feelings. The entry dated May 26, 1805, captures Lewis' feelings as his party stood in Montana viewing the Rocky Mountains for the first time. "These points of the Rocky Mountains were covered with snow, and the sun shone on it in such a manner as to give me the most plain and satisfactory view while I viewed these mountains. I felt a secret pleasure in finding myself so near the head to the hereto considered boundless Missouri River. But when I reflected on the difficulty which this snowy barrier would most probably throw in my way to the Pacific and the sufferings and hardships of myself and party in them, it in some measure counterbalanced the joy I had felt in the first moments in which I gazed on them (but I have always held it a crime to anticipate evils). I will believe it a good and comfortable road until I am compelled to believe differently."

The entry entitled "Indian Encounter" captures the sense of ambassadorship that he had on the long journey: "Children. The great chief of the 17 great nations of America, impelled by his parental regard for his newly adopted children on the troubled waters, has sent us out to clear the road. He has commanded us, his chiefs, to undertake this long journey. You are to live in peace with all white men, for they are his children. Neither wage war against the red men, your neighbors, for they are equally his children, and he is bound to protect them. Injure not the person of any traders that come among you. Do these things which your great father advises and be happy. Avoid the council of bad birds, turn your heel from them as you would from the precipice of a high rock, lest by one false step you should bring upon your nation the displeasure of your great father . . . who could consume you as fire consumes the grass of the plains."

—Dan Benuska

Monday of Holy Week   *Stewardship*

JOHN 12:1-11

Stewardship from Death's Perspective

We can offer a million reasons and a million excuses to justify what we give or don't give to the Lord. I wonder what it would take to get through to us. Earl Willer tells the story of two men that had met together, one for the purpose of asking the other to make a pledge to the church, the other to answer the request. The man asked to make a pledge said: "It seems to me all the church ever does is ask for money, money, money, that's all they want."

The man seeking the pledge answered him and said, "When my son was a little boy, he was costly; he always wanted boots and shoes, stockings and clothes, and wore them out faster than I was seemingly able to provide. The older he grew the more money had to be spent on him. But now he hasn't cost me a penny for more than a year." "How's that?" inquired the first. "Well, he died," responded the second.[1]

I wonder if the disciples would have complained about the costly gift given to Jesus if they had realized the short time He had left with them? I wonder if the disciples felt they had given enough as they stood around Him at Golgotha? He had, after all, given everything for them.

[1] Earl C. Willer, *A Treasury of Inspirational Illustrations,* (Grand Rapids, Mich.: Baker Book House, © 1975)

—Dan Benuska

Tuesday of Holy Week   *Cross/Power*

JOHN 12:20-36

Surrender to God's Will

We grow weary and are frequently tempted to throw in the towel. But the cross says to us that there is something in the world stronger and deeper than the things that succeed, namely, the things that fail, the things that are right and that honorably and sacrificially fail. Surrender to the will of God and service to people are the things that finally are victorious. This is why George Tyrell, fighting a hard battle for the truth against many enemies, once wrote: "Again and again I have been tempted to give up the struggle, but always the figure of that strange Man hanging on the cross sends me back to my task again." He does that for us every Sunday, does He not, and whenever during the week we think of Him? The cross preaches to us the potency of a life that cares enough about people to die for them. And "if it dies, it bears much fruit" (John 12:24).

—Herbert F. Lindemann, "The Mystery of the Cross," in *The Cross in Agony and Ecstasy* (St. Louis: Concordia, 1973), pp. 57—58.

Wednesday of Holy Week   *Betrayal/Forgiveness*

MATTHEW 26:14-25

The Many Forms of Betrayal

Judas speaks:

"He knew what I would do. Even when we celebrated the Passover in that rented upper hall, He knew. I could see it in His eyes. And then He said, 'One of you will betray Me!' I was nervous. I didn't want to give myself away, but the disciples persisted in asking Him who it might be. He said, 'He who has dipped his hands in the dish with Me will betray Me.' . . .

"I won't deny I betrayed Jesus . . . Can you deny that you have betrayed Him? As long as (you) hate, you betray the One who loves. As long as you deceive each other and cheat one another . . . as long as you maim and murder . . . you betray Him. As long as you make money your chief object of affection, and social position your main goal in life you are like me. Together we betray the One they call the Christ. . . .

". . . You're all like me. Don't deny it! I alone stand out as chief betrayer, however, for I forgot what the Lord Christ taught. I should have known that even one such as I could be forgiven. I was possessed by a Satanic force more evil than I can say. It blinded me from so much, but you have the chance to see. Yes, we're not so different. We all have betrayed Him, yet you have a chance to meet Love's power and know the cleansing might of forgiveness. Or have you, too, missed that truth?"

—Richard Anderson, "Judas," in *Living Lenten Portraits* (St. Louis: Concordia, 1975)

Maundy Thursday   *Upper Room/Holy Communion*

MARK 14:12-26

Proclaim the Lord's Death

Many years have passed since that first Maundy Thursday when the first disciples ate of that heavenly supper with their Lord. Since that time countless Christians have received the comfort and strength of this Holy Communion with their Lord and with each other in their own day. The Upper Room is ever a present-day room to the believer. When Leonardo da Vinci painted the *Last Supper,* he placed that incident from the life of our Lord into a contemporary setting. Under the magic of his brush, the Upper Room becomes an Italian dining hall. The Master and His disciples take their places at a Renaissance table. Tonight, as we are gathered here to eat and to drink with Him, this 20th-century church is transformed into the Upper Room. The same Host is here. Disciples are here. You are among them. You hear His words, "This is My body, which is given for you . . . My blood which is shed for you. . . ."

—Erich H. Heintzen, "Were You There When He Gave His Holy Supper?" in *Were You There?* (St. Louis: Concordia, 1958), pp. 57—58

Good Friday   *Rescue/Victory*

JOHN 19:17-30

"He Was Wounded for Our Transgressions"

A member of a mountain climbing rescue team, at great peril to himself, carefully worked himself down a steep precipice to reach an injured climber far below. After caring for his wounds and binding him to the rope, he guided the lifting of the injured man up the long face of the cliff to safety. When the rescuer himself at last reached the top, he cried, "I finished it!" Those words were not spoken dejectedly or despairingly. Exhausted though he was and tense from the excitement, there was a note of victory in his voice.

Though Jesus was exhausted and in agony on the cross, His "It is finished!" was not spoken in resignation and despair. For Jesus by His dying rescued us from the abyss of sin and the cleft of hell. He finished doing that. That's why His words are a cry of victory and exultation.

The Resurrection of Our Lord   *Unaware/God's Presence*

JOHN 20:1-9 (10-18)

Alleluia, Jesus Lives!

We are like our forefathers who lived all their days in a world containing the marvel of electricity, and yet they never guessed that it was there. Or we are like the man with the rake

47

in Bunyan's dream, gazing permanently downwards, so obsessed with his task of gathering the sticks and straws and dust off the floor that he never noticed, standing behind him, a shining figure with a celestial crown held forth in his hand. We are so apt to be obsessed with the sticks and straws of our own weak efforts of will, ineffectual resolves, and insubstantial longings: never dreaming that the Lord God who resurrected Christ is standing beside us, with that gift of supernatural power—ours, if we would but take it!

—James S. Stewart, "The Power of His Resurrection," in *King Forever,*
(Nashville: Abingdon, 1975), p.148

Second Sunday of Easter   *Scars/Victory*

JOHN 20:19-31

The Victory That Overcomes the World

"Scarred men come for healing only to scarred Hands! Only a Risen Jesus with scars can understand our hearts. This is not an age of wars, but an age of scars! We all have scars! Everybody! Scars on bodies—the wounds of war; scars on souls—the wounds of godlessness. Scars of hate, fear, anxiety, melancholy, bitterness! Either scars fighting against Thee or scars fighting with Thee! Scars born of the offensive against Love; scars born of the defense of Love!

"Come, Jesus of the Scars, I am not strong, until Thy pierced Hand clasps my own; I am not brave till I see the pledge of victory on Thy Heart; and I am not free, till Thou dost bind me to Thy Scars!"

—Fulton J. Sheen, "Easter," in *The Twentieth Century Pulpit* (Nashville: Abingdon, 1978), p. 206

Third Sunday of Easter   *Faith/Word*

LUKE 24:36-49

Faith Illuminates

The disciples could never have been persuaded to believe that the dead Jesus had risen from the grave if they had not believed His Word. Even the empty grave did not bring the disciples to faith. Only after Jesus opened the Scriptures to them did the scales fall from their eyes and did they realize how many dotted lines in the life of the Savior pointed to and intersected at this point where the event of Easter burst upon them. It was as if hitherto they had seen the colored windows in the sanctuary of this unique life only from the outside. The panes were dark and the language of the pictures was obscure. But when, by the Word, they were transported to the interior of this mystery, the pictures sprang into life and took on sight and speech. What had seemed gray to them before, the mute, empty meaninglessness of which had plunged them into the panic of Golgotha and caused them to doubt everything, now became for them an eloquent and compelling sign. Suddenly they realized that He had come from the eternity of the Father to share for a little while their life on earth.

—Adapted from Helmut Thielicke, "Living by the Resurrection," in
Christ and the Meaning of Life, (Grand Rapids: Baker, 1975)

Fourth Sunday of Easter   *Feeling Unimportant/*
Important to Christ

JOHN 10:11-18

Are You Not Much Greater Than They?

Some time ago I visited in the hospital with a man who was recuperating from a fall in which he had broken his leg. But he didn't think he was recuperating. When the cast which had been on his leg for two months was removed, he was not able to move his leg at all. Now, after almost a month of whirlpool baths and exercise, he could move it only a little. The man was sure he would never walk again. He felt that the hospital personnel didn't really care about him. He thought he was of no importance to anyone. He was despondent to the point of wishing he could die.

We have all felt at times that we were of no importance to anyone. That feeling may have resulted from tension at home, difficulty with people on our job, or frustration at school. Whatever the cause, we had to struggle to maintain an image of our own self-worth.

Our text speaks to this matter of overcoming feelings of worthlessness. Christ Himself assures us that we are individually very important to Him.

—Gerhard Aho

Fifth Sunday of Easter   *Leaves/United to Christ*

JOHN 15:1-8

Strength from His Strength

We are all like leaves on a tree. We are alike in many ways. God created all of us. We all have bodies and souls. We all share the experience of being people.

Each of us is also different from the others. We come in different colors, shapes, and sizes. But the big difference among people is our relationship to Christ. Some are connected to Christ like those leaves you see on that tree outside the window. Others are separated from Christ—like this leaf I'm holding in my hand is separated from the tree.

The big difference between the leaf that has been removed from the tree and the leaves on the tree is that the ones still on the tree can continue to receive strength from the tree. When we are united to Christ by faith, we can continue to receive His power for our life and "bear much fruit."

—Adapted from Eldon Weisheit, "Remain United with Me," in *The Gospel for Kids, Series B* (St. Louis: Concordia, 1978)

Sixth Sunday of Easter   *Love's Influence/Love*

JOHN 15:9-17

As the Twig Is Bent ...

More than 50 years ago at Johns Hopkins University in Baltimore, a young sociology professor assigned his class to a city slum to interview 200 boys. "On the basis of your findings, predict their future," he said.

Shocked at what they found in the slums, the students estimated that 90 percent of the boys interviewed would someday serve time in prison.

Twenty-five years passed. The same professor asked another class to try to locate the survivors of the 200 boys and compare what had happened. Of 180 of the original boys located, only four had ever been in jail.

Why had the predictions not turned out? A common denominator was sought in their lives, some value or influence that may have marked the difference. Through more interviews, it was found that over 100 of the men remembered having the same high school teacher, a Miss O'Rourke, who had been a tremendous influence on them at the time. After a long search, Sheila O'Rourke, now 70 years old, was found in a nursing home in Memphis. When asked for her explanation, she was puzzled. "All I can say," she concluded, "is that I loved everyone of them."

—Robert J. Hastings, *Hastings Illustrations* (Nashville: Broadman, 1971)

The Ascension of Our Lord — *Lifted Hands/Ascension*

LUKE 24:44-53

The Lord Bless . . .

The ascension of Christ has been indelibly stamped on my mind by means of a painting that hung over the altar of the church I attended as a boy. The painting depicts Christ rising from the earth, with the disciples gazing up at Him in wonder. Whenever I looked at that painting, my eyes were drawn to the hands of Jesus. They were extended upward, and I could even see on His hands the scars of the nails. Evidently the artist had paid close attention to Luke's words: "And lifting up His hands, He blessed them. While He blessed them, He parted from them."

Although Jesus must have lifted up His hands at other times during His earthly ministry, the only time the New Testament writers mention the lifting up of His hands is in connection with His ascension. Perhaps that is significant. There is a message for us in the lifted hands of the ascending Lord.

—Gerhard Aho

Seventh Sunday of Easter — *Sand Traps/World*

JOHN 17:11b-19

Surmounting the World's Difficulties

Golfers rightly fear the hazards of sand traps, yet few can avoid them completely. At some time our course in life will catch us in the adversity of a sand trap. The danger is that we may be unprepared to deal with the tough situations in life.

Arnold Palmer, the famous golf champion, said on one occasion that over the years he had watched hundreds of golfers practicing. He had observed them meticulously practicing putting—the short putts on the soft velvet grass—and he had watched them practice the swing down the fairway, but in all his lifetime and experience, he had never once seen a golfer practicing how to get out of a sand trap.

Jesus said, "In the world you have tribulation; but be of good cheer, I have overcome the world" (John 16:33). For the Christian, there is a way out—"I can do all things in Him who strengthens me" (Phil. 4:13).

—Benjamin P. Browne, *Illustrations for Preaching* (Nashville: Broadman, 1977)

The Day of Pentecost — *Spiritual Craving/Thirst*

JOHN 7:37-39a

My Soul Thirsts for You!

While traveling through the inland of Australia in 1956, where temperatures exceeded 115° and where there were no lakes, streams, or even puddles for miles on end, I could imagine the plight of a person whose supply of water failed. As late as the opening decades of this century, it was not uncommon for men to perish from thirst in the parched outback of the vast continent down under.

Today, dying of thirst happens about as rarely in Australia as in the United States. If we need water, we can usually get it.

There is another kind of thirst, however, one of the mind and heart. When a person yearns to understand the purpose of his individual life, when he craves peace within—when a person has this kind of thirst, we have to do with a problem that lies at the root of our existence, at the center of our reason for being. For just as we cannot live by bread alone, so we cannot live by physical water alone. The crucial question then is, What are we going to do about spiritual thirst?

—Gerhard Aho

The Holy Trinity
(First Sunday After Pentecost)

Spirit Draws Through Witness

JOHN 3:1-17

"You Shall Be Witnesses" . . .

Charles Colson and his friend Fred went to a small restaurant for lunch. They both bowed their heads and Fred led in a prayer—out loud. When he finished and they raised their heads, the waitress was standing near by and watching.

"Hey, were you guys praying?" she seemed surprised and asked her question so loud that everyone in the small room turned to look.

"YES!"

"That's neat. I've never seen anybody do that in here before. Are you preachers?"

"No, not really. But we work in the same business."

A lot of discussion followed and the waitress admitted, "I was a Christian—when I was a teenager. But I lost interest."

They talked more and finally the waitress volunteered. "Funny thing. A girl friend of mine has been wanting me to go to this Bible study group with her. Now I think I will."

Some time later in the same restaurant, the waitress eagerly told of her experience in the Bible study group and said that she was looking for a church. "I've come back. Thanks, guys."

—Charles Colson, *Life Sentence,* Chosen Books, 1979, pp. 105—6

Second Sunday After Pentecost

Blue Laws

MARK 2:23-28

The Demands of the Law

Under the blue laws of the 17th and 18th centuries Puritans administered religion to unwilling subjects by means of the whipping post, the ducking stool, the stocks, fines, and prisons. Mrs. Alice Morse Earle's history, *The Sabbath in Puritan New England,* lists such examples:

Two lovers, John Lewis and Sarah Chapman, were accused and tried for sitting together on the Lord's day under an apple tree.

A Dunstable soldier, for wetting a piece of old hat to put in his shoe to protect his foot, was fined forty shillings for doing this heavy work.

Captain Kemble of Boston in 1656 was put in public stocks for two hours for his "lewd and unseemly behavior" which consisted of kissing his wife in public on the Sabbath on the doorstep of his house after his return from a three-year voyage.

A man who had fallen into the water absented himself from church to dry his only suit of clothes; he was found guilty and publicly whipped.

—As quoted in "The Blue Laws of New England," *Liberty,* January-February 1963, pp. 18—19.

Third Sunday After Pentecost

Repatterning Life

MARK 3:20-35

Christ's Design for Life

Lloyd J. Ogilvie, pastor of First Presbyterian Church in Hollywood, tells of the moving experience of working with a boy who had suffered severe brain damage in an automobile accident. The only hope for him to walk and run again was through what the doctors called a repatterning of his brain. For several hours each day children of the neighborhood would take turns working the little boy's arms and legs. The doctor explained that this way new grooves were being formed in the brain which would eventually enable the boy to use the limbs on his own power.

Pastor Ogilvie says, "I'll never forget the excitement we all felt when that boy began to regain his ability to walk and play." Then he reflects on the task of the church, to help people of God repattern their brains so that they can run according to God's plan for His people in the world.
—"The Church Needs Repatterning," *Faith at Work,* August 1973

Fourth Sunday After Pentecost   *The Seed Grows*

MARK 4:24-26

Sharing the Word

As we visited the Khoa I Dang refugee camps on the border between Thailand and Kampuchea (Cambodia) our guide, an official of World Relief, who worked closely with the administration of the camp, explained the helpless situation of the 120,000 people living in the cramped bamboo thatched huts. They couldn't go back to their homes because of the Khmer Rouge guerrillas; they were not eligible for resettlement. But the guide explained that God is at work among them.

A Christian pastor with 200 of his members had come with the stream of refugees from Kampuchea and with the aid of some missionaries had built a bamboo church in the camp. They had started Bible classes throughout the week in different areas of the camp. On Sunday the church overflowed and 5,000 people stood around outside listening to the sermon over a public address system.

In conclusion the guide explained that there were more Christians in that one camp that day than there were in all of Cambodia before the war—after 50 years of missionary work there.
—Erwin J. Kolb

Fifth Sunday After Pentecost   *Guilty*

MARK 4:35-41

"Whoso Shall Offend in One Point" . . .

Browsing through the produce section of a Kroger's store in Montgomery, W. Va., Mirhadi Seyedashraf, a senior studying engineering at the West Virginia Institute of Technology, picked up one white seedless grape to test it. Very quickly the young Iranian learned that the casual shopping habits of the market stalls of his country were not those of suspicious American supermarkets. He was arrested on a shoplifting charge.

It didn't matter whether he took one grape, one bunch of grapes or a bushel of them. The amount was not the issue but the fact that he had stolen.

The Lord says that if we break one commandment, even in our thoughts, we have broken the entire law and are guilty.
—*Time,* August 4, 1980, p. 26

Sixth Sunday After Pentecost   *The Assurance of Life*

MARK 5:21-24a, 35-43

"Fear Not, I Am with You!"

Dr. C. A. Van Andel, chairman of the Department of Internal Medicine at Muskegon General Hospital, Muskegon, Mich., tells of his experiences in dealing with patients who suddenly face some serious illness and now for the first time in their lives think of the possibility of death. Perhaps they have had good health all their lives, but now they confront serious surgery, a heart attack, or cancer.

It is common, he says, to see a real sense of fear and apprehension. Many of them have been exposed to Christianity through a church or by radio or television, but they have never taken the time to think through their personal relationship with God and their eternal destiny. In talking to these patients, Dr. Van Andel often asks, "Are you prepared to meet God?" Answers vary: "I hope so," "I think so," and in some cases "Yes, I know so." What constitutes the difference?

The difference lies in whether the patient bases his answer on the proper authority. Medical textbooks are the authority for medical answers. The Bible, the Word of God, is the authority for spiritual needs. When a person sees his spiritual condition and understands his need for rescue from spiritual death, he needs to hear his authority say:

"For the wages of sin is death, but the gift of God is eternal life."

—C. A. Van Andel, American Bible Society Tract, "I hope so, I think so, Yes, I know so!"

Seventh Sunday After Pentecost   *Blinded*

MARK 6:1-6

Follow Him Implicitly

"Can you see the flag? Is it still there?" an anxious voice asked Francis Scott Key as he trained his field glasses on beleaguered Fort McHenry in Baltimore Harbor. It was September 14, 1814, and they had watched all night during the bombardment. As the dawn crept in and a breeze cleared away some of the mist and smoke, they saw it. The flag was still there.

That evening in his hotel room, Francis Scott Key took the notes he had made during the night-long watch and wrote a poem which began with the question: "O say can you see?"

Francis Scott Key was an attorney in Georgetown, a patriot, and a believer in Jesus Christ as his Lord and Savior. His letters reveal what kind of man he was. In one letter he wrote to his cousin: "Nothing but Christianity will give you victory. . . . Fix the firmest conviction of its truth in your understanding, study its evidences, establish its principles in your heart. . . . Until a man believes in his heart that Jesus is His Lord and Master and joins in the earnest and eloquent application of the convert's prayer, 'Lord what will you have me to do?' his course through life will neither be safe nor pleasant. . . . My only regret now is that I was so long *blinded by my pleasures, my vices and pursuits, and the examples of others* from seeing, admiring, and adoring the marvelous light of the Gospel. . . ."

—Edward S. Delaplaine, *Francis Scott Key: Life and Times,* as quoted in
"The Star Spangled Banner," *Decision,* July 1980

Eighth Sunday After Pentecost   *Justified*

MARK 6:7-13

Declared Righteous

A Sunday school teacher had done her best to explain the meaning of the word "justified" as it is so frequently used in the King James version of the Bible in Christian code language. In her review questions on the following Sunday, she asked, "Does anyone remember what the Bible means when it says that we've been 'justified' by God?"

There was an awkward silence. Then a timid boy answered, "When the Bible says I'm justified," he fumbled, "it means that, no matter what I've done bad, God is willing to look at me just-if-I'd never done it—'cause Jesus died for me."

—Herman Gockel, *Portals of Prayer,* July 18, 1980

Ninth Sunday After Pentecost   *Compassion Leads to Action*

MARK 6:30-34

Redeem Your Brother?

Al Quie, who for 20 years was a respected member of Congress from the State of Minnesota, and later became governor of that state, was deeply moved when his friend Charles Colson and brother in Christ was sentenced to prison for his involvement in the Watergate coverup. He struggled to find a way in which he could help. Finally in the law books, he found a little known statute that permits one man to serve the prison term of another. All of his life he had suffered from a fear of being imprisoned—ever since he had been taken as a third grader to visit a local jail. But here was something he could do for his brother. He telephoned and offered to take Colson's place and serve the sentence for him. And he would have, if Colson had not refused.

—Charles Colson, *Born Again*

Tenth Sunday After Pentecost   *Giver of Food*

JOHN 6:1-15

"The Eyes of All" . . .

An 800-page study issued by a presidential panel warns that the food supply is running out and unless some drastic measures are taken we are headed for a global catastrophe. By the year 2000 at current and projected birth rates, the population will have risen from the 5 billion of 1975 to 6.35 billion with most of the growth taking place in the poorer, less developed countries of the world, mostly in their urban slums and shantytowns.

The report paints a gloomy picture. While food production will rise 90 percent over the 1970 levels, most of the increase will go to the countries that are already well fed. So, the number of malnourished in the world will rise to a billion and a half. Starvation will claim an increasing number of babies. Many of the survivors will grow up physically and mentally stunted. There will be increasing illness and misery.

Where do we look for the solution? The report can only point to solutions that are "complicated and long-term, . . . inextricably linked to some of the most perplexing and persistent problems in the world—poverty, injustice, and social conflict." Can't we also look to the One who fed 5,000 with a few loaves and fishes?

—*Time,* August 4, 1980, p. 54

Eleventh Sunday After Pentecost   *The Bread That Strengthens*

JOHN 6:24-35

Seek First the Kingdom of God

An Eskimo fisherman came to town every Saturday afternoon with two dogs, one white and the other black. He had taught them to fight on command. People would gather in the town square for the fight each week, and the fisherman would take their bets as to which one would win. One Saturday, the black dog would win; another Saturday the white dog would win. But the fisherman always knew which one would win and so won the bets.

How did he know which dog was going to win each week? The time came when he revealed his secret to his friends. "I starve one and feed the other. The one that I feed always wins because he is stronger."

There are two natures in man. The one that is fed is stronger and wins.

—Billy Graham, *The Holy Spirit*

Twelfth Sunday After Pentecost   *How to Die*

JOHN 6:41-51

Prepared to Meet Your God

During World War I a party was given for a group of soldiers soon to go to the front. Near the close of the evening, a young officer rose to express appreciation for the entertainment. His remarks were cheerful, full of charm and humor. Then, suddenly, as an afterthought before sitting down, using a different tone of voice, he said, "We are soon crossing to France... and very possibly, of course, to death. Will any one of our friends here tell us how to die?"

There was a stunned silence. It seems that no one knew what to say. Finally, one of the singers who had taken part in the program came forward and turning to the soldier, began to sing the great aria from Mendelssohn's *Elijah:*

> O rest in the Lord, wait patiently for Him,
> And He shall give thee thy heart's desires;
> Commit thy way unto Him, and trust in Him;
> And fret not thyself because of evil-doers.
> O rest in the Lord, wait patiently for Him,
> And He shall give thee thy heart's desires.

—G. Ray Jordan, *The Supreme Possession* (New York: Abingdon-Cokesbury, 1945), p. 186 f.

Thirteenth Sunday After Pentecost   *Already Died*

JOHN 6:51-58

Lose the Body?

Henri Nouwen tells of a Lutheran bishop who was imprisoned in a German concentration camp during World War II and beaten by an SS officer in order to extract a confession from him about his political action. The beatings continued to increase in intensity, but the bishop maintained his silence. Finally, the infuriated officer shrieked, "Don't you know that I can kill you?"

The bishop looked in the eyes of his torturer and said, "Yes, I know—do what you want—but I have already died."

Instantly as though paralyzed, the officer could no longer raise his arm. It was as if power over the bishop had been taken from him. All his cruelties had been based on the assumption that the bishop's physical life was his most precious possession and therefore he would be willing to make any concession to save it. But with the grounds for violence gone, torture was futile.

—*Henri J. M. Nouwen, Reaching Out: The Three Movements of Spiritual Life* (New York: Doubleday, 1975), p. 84

Fourteenth Sunday After Pentecost   *Word Gives Life*

JOHN 6:60-69

Accomplishing His Purpose

Paul was a drug addict and an alchoholic, and he had to steal in order to pay for his expensive habit. He stole whatever he could get his hands on. One of his targets was cars that were left unlocked, or had windows rolled down. One day in such a car he found nothing but a book on the back seat. It probably wouldn't buy a "fix," but it would at least give him something to read between drinks. So he took it.

The book had a red and black cover with the single word title, "Jesus." It was an American Bible Society edition of the Gospel words of Jesus. He read it. But the full significance of what he read did not sink in immediately. Some time later, two young men asked him if he had heard about Jesus.

"Yeah, I read a book about Him," he said. As the conversation continued, he became more interested and began asking questions. After more reading and conversation, Paul became an eager disciple of Jesus Christ. His life was changed, and he began to share his new life with others. Today he is in a seminary studying for the ministry and still wondering who left the book about "Jesus" on the back seat of his car.

—American Bible Society Record, June-July, 1980

Fifteenth Sunday After Pentecost   *Inner Purity*

MARK 7:1-8, 14-15, 21-23

Life Is Preserved by Inner Purity

"Urban Ghosts: Bag Ladies of New York" is the title of a feature article written by Christopher Evans (Minneapolis *Star* writer) and illustrated with the shocking photos of Stormi Greener. In it, Evans describes the plight of the "bag ladies," or "skels"—for skeletons—who literally live on the sidewalks of New York, carrying all of their possessions in shopping bags. All are ragged and umkempt, some are sick, and others are covered with sores. They remind a person of the "unclean"—the lepers and social outcasts of Jesus' day. The tensions and cruelties of life seem to be destroying them.

Anna is one of the "bag ladies." Her plight is pitiful. She stays close to the Church of St. Francis of Assisi where "the food wagon stops (every morning) and distributes two stale bologna sandwiches and a cup of coffee to anyone in line." Evans says: "She doesn't walk, she slides, all hunched over. She covers herself in layers of burlap, pulls on an old raincoat, then a sweater, and opens an umbrella. Her hands are badly arthritic, gnarled like old wood. She smells very bad, has no teeth; sometimes it seems she is folding her whole face into her mouth." Anna is a victim of the worst that life and people can do to someone.

But Anna has not been completely destroyed by the evil forces of life. A spark of hope is bright within her because, Evans notes, she is still able to say, "I wish you could have seen me when I was clean." Outwardly, she is almost a derelict but, inwardly, she is still alive and pure.

Sixteenth Sunday After Pentecost   *Opening Ears*

MARK 7:31-37

Hearing Leads to Speaking

Matthew was six months old when our neighbors brought him home from the adoption agency. He was sickly and small for his age. It was obvious that he had been neglected and might have health and growth problems. As he grew, it was feared that he might be retarded; he was much older than average before he began to speak and walk. Matthew seldom smiled or laughed; he seemed to be living almost in a world of his own.

When Matthew was 3½ or 4 years old, his parents took him to medical specialists on advice of their pediatrician. Diagnostic procedures revealed that his speech and personality problems were related to poor vision and limited hearing ability. He was fitted with a hearing aid and glasses and, once he became acclimated to these devices, his speech began to improve and his personality began to develop. For the first time since he was born he could see and hear—and a whole new world opened up for him. It was much like that with the deaf and dumb man to whom Jesus said, "Be opened!" Nothing could keep him quiet—about Jesus' gift to him—after that.

Through Word and Spirit, Jesus opens our hearts and minds to the miracle of God's love—and we are free to speak of the wonders of that love.

—George Bass

Seventeenth Sunday After Pentecost   *Self-Denial/Service*

MARK 8:27-35

Total Commitment to Christ

An incident in the life of Pablo Casals illuminates the nature of the total commitment that Christ demands of his followers. U Thant held a reception for the famous musician when he was 94 years of age. Robert Muller, in his *Most of All, They Taught Me Happiness*, describes how he was talking with Casals in a room on the 38th floor of the United Nations Secretariat building when a waitress came by with filled glasses. In the bright light, Casals asked, "What is it?" She answered, with a smile, "Lemonade." Before he could taste it, his wife intercepted the glass and tasted it: "This is champagne! You cannot drink it."

Muller says, "Thereupon Pablo Casals told me the following story: 'When I was a young man, I once went to see my doctor and told him I was feeling a kind of laziness in my fingers. After a thorough examination, he asked me: "Do you drink?" I answered negatively, but added that like all Spaniards I had a glass of wine at luncheon and at dinner. He then said: "Well, if you want to become a great, renowned artist and avoid that laziness in your fingers, you must never touch a drop of wine or alcohol." I obeyed him faithfully all my life.' "

Eighteenth Sunday After Pentecost   *Servanthood*

MARK 9:30-37

To Understand the Gospel Is to Serve

The young man—wearing a clerical collar—on the hospital elevator was not yet 25 years old; he looked as young as he was. A woman entered, noticed his clerical attire, and looked a bit puzzled. As the elevator ascended, she continued to stare at him and finally blurted out, "Are you a priest, or something?" He explained to her that he was a Lutheran seminarian doing his third year internship in a local parish. That silenced her until the elevator reached her floor, but as she was about to go out the door, she turned to him once more and said, "I didn't know that people your age did that sort of thing any more." With that, she went her way.

People in our parishes know that God still calls young people—and that many who are called answer and enter seminary. They are also aware of the model Christ established for the ministry, according to the research of the Search Institute in Minneapolis. The trait that laypeople most desire in their future pastors is "willingness to serve without acclaim." Jesus said, "If anyone would be first, he must be last of all and servant of all." And that means all Christians—lay people and clergy alike.

—George Bass

Nineteenth Sunday After Pentecost   *Warning to Child-Seducers*

MARK 9:38-50

Seduction of the Innocent

William Murray, son of the atheist Madalyn Murray O'Hair and the plaintiff in the

57

1963 lawsuit that ended prayer in the public schools, has said that he feels personally responsible for the "destruction of the moral fiber" of American youth. Neil Postman, author of *Teaching as a Conserving Activity,* would disagree; he believes that television, as the "primary curriculum" in life today, is the seducer of the innocent. Surveys and studies tend to bear him out and affirm his conclusions.

A survey conducted for the Foundation for Child Development by Temple University's Institute for Survey Research revealed that "millions of American children live in fear, caused by TV viewing. . . . " Two-thirds of the 2,200 children interviewed were fearful that "somebody bad" might break into their homes. One fourth of them were afraid that "someone would hurt them" if they went outside to play. Over half of them were afraid when their parents had an argument. Dr. Orville G. Brim, president of the foundation, says that federal action is needed to protect children from the negative effects (fear and other effects) of TV. He said, ". . . millions of children watch anything they want on television, any time." Parents who permit such indiscriminate viewing contribute to the problem.

Twentieth Sunday After Pentecost — *Holy Matrimony*

MARK 10:2-16

Marriage and Divorce

A now-discarded marriage service began, "Marriage is a holy estate, ordained by God, and to be held in honor by all." Not only do most contemporary services omit statements like this, they also provide opportunity for couples to compose their own marriage vows which often fall short of the Biblical injunction, "So they are no longer two but one flesh. What therefore God has joined together, let not man put asunder." Divorce is almost built-into the marriage ceremony with vows that change "as long as we shall live" into "as long as we love each other." Marriage is sacred because it is a creation of God, not merely a human institution lightly to be discarded. Love, faithfulness, forgiveness, and self-sacrifice are its essence and, at the same time, evidence of God's gift in marriage.

In "The Bird and the Machine," Loren Eiseley tells how he once captured a sparrow hawk, whose mate escaped when the male hawk clawed him and bit his thumb. The next morning, when he was supposed to load the young hawk into a truck for a trip to a zoo, something moved him to put the hawk down on the ground. The young hawk had looked up at the bright sky while he was being held. On the ground, he continued to look up into the bright light. Suddenly he vanished and, shortly, " . . . from far up somewhere a cry came ringing down." Eiseley says, "When I heard that cry my heart turned over." It was the cry of his mate who must have been soaring for hours, " . . . ringing from peak to peak of the summits over us, . . . a cry of such unutterable and ecstatic joy that it sounds down across the years and tingles among the cups on my quiet breakfast table."

"I saw them both now," Eiseley recalls. "He was rising fast to meet her. They met in a great soaring gyre that turned to a whirling circle and a dance of wings. Once more, just once, their two voices, joined in a harsh wild medley of question and response, struck and echoed against the pinnacles of the valley. Then they were gone forever somewhere into those upper regions beyond the eyes of men." Perhaps the birds teach us a lesson about God's creation—marriage—and the gifts that make it holy.

> —From *The Immense Journey,* and republished in Eiseley's self-chosen, posthumously published collection, *The Star Thrower.*

Twenty-First Sunday After Pentecost — *Wealth/Stewardship*

MARK 10:17-27 (28-30)

Stewardship, Not Renunciation, Counts

Totino's was a Minneapolis restaurant, begun in the 1950s, specializing in Italian food.

Their pizza was so well received that by 1962 Totino's had entered the wholesale pizza business. In a few years the business survived difficult times and began to develop a nationwide reputation for excellence. Just a few years ago, Totino's was purchased by the Pillsbury Co. for $20.3 million dollars, and Mrs. Totino became the first woman vice-president of the Pillsbury administration. Financial problems were at an end for Mr. and Mrs. Totino; they were wealthy.

But the story does not end there, as it might have. On the day that the Totino-Pillsbury sale was consummated, Mrs. Totino gave $2 million dollars to Northwestern College, a small Bible-college in St. Paul, out of gratitude for its radio ministry which, she claims, changed her life. Her husband, a Roman Catholic (she is Protestant), made a similar gift to a local Catholic high school. The Totinos continue, more than half a decade later, to give away their wealth—in the name of Jesus Christ.

Twenty-Second Sunday After Pentecost *Jesus' Baptism*

MARK 10:35-45

Baptism in Blood

Jesus was baptized twice—with water, by John the Baptizer, in the Jordan River, and with blood, by His enemies, on the cross at Golgotha. As He predicted, many of His followers were baptized with blood as well as water. The "blood of the martyrs" flowed freely—and still does—in witness to the Gospel and evidence of faith. One realizes this more fully in Rome than anywhere else in the world, with its more than a thousand churches bearing the names of the saints and martyrs of antiquity. The original saints were all martyrs or confessors—not workers of miracles—and they constitute a "noble army" indeed.

Most tourists visit the Catacombs of St. Sebastian on the Appian Way, but unless they are alert, they don't make the connection between the paintings of this martyr found in art galleries all over the world and the catacomb, or the church on top of it. Sebastian was executed—placed before an arrow-firing squad of Roman soldiers—and, when dead, was buried in this place. The bodies of Peter and Paul might have been hidden there when he was buried; they, too, were placed there temporarily during times of persecution. But it was the bloody death of Sebastian, a young Christian officer in the Roman army, who refused to renounce his faith in Christ, that intrigued the multitude of artists of the Middle Ages and influenced the church to give his name to the underground cemetery and church. The holy catholic church honors the martyrs simply because they have been baptized with Christ's baptism at Calvary.

—George Bass

Twenty-Third Sunday After Pentecost *Christ Cares*

MARK 10:46-52

Caring Enough to Stop

When Jesus heard a blind man crying out, "Jesus, Son of David, have mercy on me!" He cared enough to stop in His tracks and to ask the man, "What do you want of Me?" It is not always that way with us and the poor, the sick, the blind, and the halt.

Colman McCarthy wrote a story about a "John Doe" who died in Washington. President Carter, a few days earlier, had told a group of religious broadcasters that "the hungry and the homeless . . . are testimony to man's capacity for evil." The story simply points to our failure to care enough about the helpless people around us. McCarthy says, "If evil was at work in the death of 'John Doe'—he was known to be a diseased drinker, about 55 or 60 years old, a danger to no one—it was the evil of looking away." Although an invitation to the funeral had been issued by the Community for Creative Nonviolence, a group of pacifists and social workers that cares for the poor, only about 30—mostly the destitute— gathered to bury John Doe. The Community had hoped for a public outpouring on behalf of the outcasts of society and, McCarthy said, "If only half of those invited actually had come—from public officials to religious leaders—tens of thousands would have been marching and mourning, crying out in anger that this waste of life be stopped."

This we know: Christ would have been there. Christ was there when they buried John Doe.

Twenty-Fourth Sunday After Pentecost   *Neighborly Love*

MARK 12:28-34

Love That Is Real

Three years after President Carter requested it in 1977, the Global 2000 Report—an 800-page document—was made public. It warns that 20 years in the future—A.D. 2000—the earth will be crowded, the planet "depleted" of resources, and "hundreds of millions of the desperately poor will have to go without adequate food and material necessity. Earth's population will increase from four billion to six billion three hundred thousand people by 2000—and "5 billion of them (will be) living marginal existences in less developed countries." Food production is "projected to be 90 percent higher in 2000 than in 1970," but this will be offset by the population growth, environmental pressures, and other problems. The report emphasized: "These are projections of what could happen if policies around the world don't change. They are not predictions. . . . "

A few weeks before this report was published, another came from Nairobi: "Severe food shortages on half of continent of Africa." Twenty-one African nations—almost half of the continent—are "gripped by severe food shortages," according to the U.N. Food and Agriculture Organization. TV news programs show people starving to death in various parts of Africa. FAO Director-General Edouard Saouma declared: "We are on the verge of simultaneous human disaster in many countries of an unprecedented character." Will Christian people—around the world and in East Africa, where they could feed themselves and even export some food—respond soon enough and with enough?

Twenty-Fifth Sunday After Pentecost   *Real Stewardship*

MARK 12:41-44

Lesson in Stewardship

The first call I made as a young pastor fresh from seminary turned out to be a lesson in stewardship. A layman in the rural congregation of my town and country parish in Pennsylvania offered to help me locate the members on my first visitation in the country. He took me down a dirt road to a once-substantial stone farmhouse; its roof was mostly gone, the walls had partially crumbled, but an old lady, Annie Miles, lived there in a single room of her ancestral home. She answered our knock on the dilapidated door and let us in. She was obviously as poor as she was ancient.

Inside the door was a wood-burning stove for heat and cooking. Opposite it was a cot, and between stood an old round table piled high with her "treasures" which were, in turn, covered by an old sheet. To the left of the door was a buffet—also laden with possessions covered by another cloth; by the opposite wall was a box with chickens in it—cats seemed everywhere. The odor was overpowering, and I'm afraid I rushed the Communion a bit and almost dashed for the door—and fresh air. But she stopped me and said, "Pastor, let me get my offering for Lutheran World Action." With that, she opened the buffet and brought out a pile of offering envelopes and insisted that I take them "to help the poor." It was that way for the six years that I took Communion to her home—always an offering for the church and the poor.

I suspect that layman—Harry Quay was his name—wanted me to learn a lesson in that first call. And I did.

—George Bass

Twenty-Sixth Sunday After Pentecost   *Preach to All*

MARK 13:1-13

An Artist Proclaims the Gospel

The surrealist painter and sculptor, Salvador Dali, gave some expression to the Gospel in his art, but it was only when Picasso died that he revealed why he attempted to proclaim the Word to the world. Louis Pelligren, chief steward of the French Line ship, the FRANCE, was with Dali aboard the ship the day Picasso died. Pelligren reported Dali's reaction to the news:

"Picasso was a Spaniard. So am I."

"Picasso was a painter. So am I."

"Picasso was a genius. So am I."

"Picasso was a Communist. I am not. So I will have a mass said for him." That kind of loving concern for others compels Christians to preach the Good News to the whole world.

Twenty-Seventh Sunday After Pentecost   *Christ's Return*

MARK 13:24-31

Promise of the Parousia

The Christians of the first centuries of the church's history expected Christ to return to the earth soon—and in the manner described by the Lord. The most ancient mosaics in Rome are found in the 4th-century Rotunda of Santa Costanza, and they depict the faith of the believers. The most important of these mosaics shows Christ seated on a throne, orb in one hand, the other raised in blessing—Peter and Paul on either side of him, the apostles and angels in the background—four streams of water gushing from the ground and forming a river lined with lush grass. Sheep feed on the grass, drink from the river, at the feet of the Lord. He sustains His own until the appointed time for His final return.

This is the dominant motif that has been placed above the altars of the churches of Western Christendom for nearly 1,600 years. The church waits for His return, even as it gathers around the Table of the Lord to participate in the foretaste of "the feast to come" through the eating of the bread and the drinking of the cup which "proclaim His death until He comes." It is most appropriate that the largest tapestry in the world—the "Christ in Glory" of Graham Sutherland—paints the same picture for people today in the new cathedral at Coventry, declaring, "He will come with great power and glory."

Last Sunday After Pentecost   *Alert and Prepared*

MARK 13:32-37

Ready for Christ's Return

Survival, Incorporated, is a California-based business that merchandises many of the items sold in sporting goods outlets, "plus the kind of supplies and equipment sought by those concerned about urban riots, power failures, foreign invasions or a collapsing economy." Everything from a radiation suit to a year's supply of prepackaged food can be purchased from Survival, Inc. The name of the business suggests its reason for existence, namely: to provide products that will enable people who are fearful of the future to be prepared for whatever might occur.

William Pier, founder and owner of the business, "is not among those who predict the end of Western civilization, a collapse of the social order, and urban marauders scouring the countryside for food"—or the end of the world—but he, too, is alert and prepared. Pier owns a 60-acre farm in southern Oregon "far from cities and out of wind currents that could otherwise blow radiation his way." He is ready to retreat to his farm when it is necessary.

Pier's customers are called "survivalists"—people who want to be ready for the future. "Most of my customers," he says, "are ordinary people: brokers, bankers, secretaries, truck drivers—people who simply want to be prepared for whatever happens."

Jesus said—about His future return and the end of things as we know them: "Be on guard! Be alert! You do not know when that time will come." But all, not a few, of us are to be ready—vigilant and prepared.

Reformation Sunday — *The Word and Power Preaching*

JOHN 8:31-36

The Liberating Power of the Word

"How would you like to see Martin Luther condemned to Hell?" That question is often put to Lutheran pastors visiting Rome by other Lutheran pastors and theologians who are better acquainted with the mysteries of Rome. Those who respond affirmatively to the query are whisked across the city to the principal church of the Society of Jesus, the Church of *Il Gesu.* They are hurried into the building and ushered to the transept on the Gospel-side and confronted with the tomb-altar of Ignatius Loyola, first leader of the Society; the altar once had a solid silver statue on top of it. Done in *lapis lazuli,* agate, rare marble, and precious and semi-precious stones, it was once valued at over $50 million dollars. A marble bas-relief in the background depicts a priest—Loyola—standing in a pulpit and pointing to a group of people. The inscription says: "Loyola condemning Luther, Calvin, and the other heretics to Hell."

The intriguing thing about this bas-relief and the church is that it was built between 1558 and 1584, spanning the Council of Trent, for a specific purpose—the proclamation of the Word through preaching! The nave had no side aisles and only six small chapels that opened directly into the nave; it was built this way so that everyone might hear the Word in the preaching there. It is claimed that every Roman Catholic church built since then has had to be built on this "open"—*preaching*—plan. And while it took Vatican II to complete and implement this intention, the Word whose power Luther had rediscovered for preaching had already done its work.

Index of Scripture Texts

Index of Topics

Gospel Lessons, Series C

by
Daniel Benuska
Donald L. Deffner
Eugene E. Schmidt
Theodore W. Schroeder

Contributors

First Sunday in Advent Through Transfiguration—Daniel A. Benuska
First Sunday in Lent Through Sixth Sunday of Easter—Theodore W. Schroeder
Ascension of Our Lord Through Eleventh Sunday After Pentecost—Donald L. Deffner
Twelfth Sunday After Pentecost Through Last Sunday in the Church Year—Eugene E.
   Schmidt

Sources—Series C

Light in the Valley, Herbert Vander Lugt, Grand Rapids, MI: Radio Bible Class, 1976, p. 85.

Gospel of Luke by William Barclay, Philadelphia: Westminster Press, 1956.

Pulpit Resources, Oxnard, CA: Vol. 8, No. 3, July, August, September 1980.

Bartlett's Quotations, Emily Morison Beck, Editor. Boston: Little, Brown and Company.
   Fourteenth Edition, 1968.

Creative Ministry, Henri J. M. Nouwen, New York: Image Books, Doubleday, 1971, p. 3.

Mountain Trailways for Youth compiled by Mrs. Charles Cowman, Grand Rapids, MI:
   Zondervan, 1975.

Pulpit Resources, Oxnard, CA: Vol. 8, No. 4, October, November, December 1980.

The Lutheran, October 19, 1979.

The Hidden Discipline, Martin Marty, St. Louis: Concordia, 1974.

"Lightning Struck," Dean Haran, *Science Digest,* May, 1981.

"Identifying Ourselves," Isaac Asimov, *Science Digest,* May, 1981.

Science Digest, May, 1981.

Luther's Works, American Edition, Table Talk, Philadelphia: Fortress Press, 1967, Vol. 54,
   p. 19.

American Heritage: "Lord Bryce," Louis Auchincloss, April/May, 1981.

The National Lutheran, "A Finnish Pastor Looks at American Lutheranism," March 1948.

Beyond Personality, C. S. Lewis, New York: Macmillan, p. 40.

Meditations for College Students, Donald L. Deffner, St. Louis: Concordia, 1961, p. 15.

The Doctrine in the Liturgy, Donald L. Deffner, St. Louis: Concordia Seminary Print Shop,
   1960, p. 16.

He Sent Leanness, David Head, New York: Macmillan, p. 19.

Being a Christian, Hans Kung, New York: Doubleday & Co., 1976.

Lectionary Preaching, John R. Brokhoff, Lima, OH: CSS Publishing Co., p. 204.

TEAM—LEA, Department & Directors of Christian Education.

First Sunday in Advent   *End Time Signs*

LUKE 21:25-36

Read the Signs, and Then . . .

Fishing for bass over the years has taught me to read the signs. When it's full moon I noticed that fish feed at night. In the spring of the year I'll fish shallow with top water lures. In the hot summer days I'll fish the deep holes with a worm rod. Reading the signs is part of our life. A stockbroker knows how to read the economic indicators; a farmer knows how to read the seasons for planting; and a salesman learns how to read people. But the signs that we are most reluctant to read are the signs of the end and of our own end. Herbert Vander Lugt relates a conversation between a man whose goals seem to be only materialistic and his perceptive friend. Surveying a large estate, he exclaimed, "If I could gain possession of this property, I'd be happy. I'd tear down that old house and build a new one. I'd keep the best wines and choicest foods available and have a high time with my buddies." "And then?" asked his friend. "Well, I'd purchase some horses for hunting and riding, and have a continual open house. I'd really enjoy life!" "And Then?" persisted his companion. "Why, I suppose I'd grow old and have to die." "AND THEN?!" Yes, read the signs, take heed, "watch at all times, praying that you may have strength to escape all these things that will take place, and to stand before the Son of Man.

  —Herbert Vander Lugt, *Light in the Valley* Grand Rapids, MI.: Radio Bible Class, 1976), p. 85
                  —Dan Benuska

Second Sunday in Advent   *Humility*

LUKE 3:1-6

Pride Goes Before the Fall

Back in Ohio, as a boy growing up, I used to go fishing with my Uncle Joe in Brunswick. Brunswick Stream was about five feet deep and a dozen feet wide. It wove in a series of S curves through a pasture. One spring day when I was fishing, another young man about the same age and size appeared on the bank opposite me. "Hey," he said, "what school do you go to?" "North Olmstead," I answered. "Are you on the track team?" he said. "Yes," I replied. "Me too, Brunswick High. I'm probably the greatest broadjumper in the state." I must have looked skeptical because he continued, "You don't believe me, do you? Well, see this stream? I'm going to jump right over it." The stream had reached its widest point here, a distance of fourteen or fifteen feet. With great show he began to warm up. He carefully counted his steps and drew a line in the mud at the bank for a takeoff point. He checked and doubled-checked his footing, then after a few false starts he took off. He ran pell-mell toward the bank, hit the takeoff point, and went sailing high into the air. I can still remember him sputtering and muttering up to his chin in water and mud right in the middle of Brunswick Stream. I remember that sight when I read the words from Isaiah quoted in our Gospel for today: "Every valley shall be filled and every mountain and hill shall be brought low." Yes, that's the way it is. Pride goes before the fall. There's no room for mountains in the kingdom of God. Those who are well, and think themselves well have no need of a physical. We know the limits of our abilities and our agilities—that is why we keep our Advent watch with humility. Thank you God for leveling and lowering us enough to stand under the cross and kneel at the manger.

—Dan Benuska

Third Sunday in Advent   *Repentance*

LUKE 3:7-18

Hard Words That Are Good Words

The Gospel for this day ends with some surprising words:

So, with many other exhortations he (John) preached good news to the people.

Now normally those words wouldn't be surprising at all. But, the preceding words of John the Baptizer are among the most pulverizing and stinging words in all the gospels. He called people snakes, a brood of vipers. God's ax was already swinging, swinging against them. Judgment was already in motion. How can such terrorizing words be called good news? If you saw a three- or four-year-old child slide a chair up to a stove and turn it on, I do not think you would stand back and say, "Isn't that cute, he's about to discover fire." No, you'd shout "Stop! Stop, before you get hurt." You would shout it loud and hard. You would say it not because you don't care, but because you do. Can you see the hard words of God as God loving us, caring for us because He doesn't want to see us get hurt. There are some places we cannot afford to be, some things we simply can't afford to do, because they'll destroy us.

Some years ago, my father's cement crew was pouring the basement floor of a house. When the back half of the basement was finished, the cement truck moved around to the front of the house. Joe, one of my father's cement finishers, came out of the basement for a breather. He stopped and leaned against the house looking down through the basement window. The cement truck backed up, hit Joe with the cement chute, snapped his back and pushed him through that basement window. Joe would never walk again. He discovered in a tragic way that there are some places where a cement finisher just can't afford to stop. There are some places where we cannot afford to stop either. It is good news for us that God does not want us to stop at certain places either. He loves us so much that He will even speak a hard word with us.

—Dan Benuska

Fourth Sunday in Advent   *Revolution*

LUKE 1:39-55

The Magnificat: The World's Most Revolutionary Document

It has been said that religion is the opiate of the people; but as Stanley Jones said, "the *Magnificat* is the most revolutionary document in the world." The *Magnificat* speaks of three of the revolutions of God:

First, "He has scattered the proud in the imagination of their hearts." That is the moral revolution. Christianity is the death of pride. Why? Because if anyone sets his life beside the life

68

of Christ, it tears the last vestiges of pride from him. In His light we see our own darkness. Standing beside Him we see how far we are from what we are called to be.

Second, "He has put down the mighty from their thrones and exalted those of low degree." That is the *social* revolution. Christianity puts an end to the world's labels and prestige. "Call no man worthless for whom Christ died." When we have realized what Christ did for each person, it is no longer possible to speak about a "Common man."

Third, "He has filled the hungry with good things, and the rich he has sent empty away." This is the *economic* revolution. A society untouched by Christ is marked by acquisition where each one is out to amass as much as he can get. When our lives and our societies are touched by Christ, no one dares to have too much while others have too little, we must get only to give away."

—adapted from *The Gospel of Luke* by William Barclay.
Philadelphia: The Westminster Press, 1956
—Dan Benuska

The Nativity of Our Lord   *Incarnation*

LUKE 2:1-20

He Entered the World with Us

Dr. John Rosen, a psychiatrist in New York City, is well known for his work with catatonic schizophrenics. Normally doctors remain separate and aloof from their patients. Dr. Rosen moves into the ward with them. He places his bed among their beds. He lives the life they must live. Day to day, he shares it. He loves them. If they don't talk, he doesn't talk either. It is as if he understands what is happening. His being there, being with them communicates something that they haven't experienced in years—somebody understands. But then he does something else. He puts his arms around them and hugs them. He holds these unattractive, unlovable, sometimes incontinent persons, and loves them back into life. Often, the first words they speak are simply "thank you."

It's obvious that this is what God did for us through Jesus at Christmas. He moved into the ward with us. He placed His bed among our beds. Those who were there, those who saw Him, touched Him and were in turn touched by Him and restored to life. The first word they had to say was "thank you."

And the shepherds returned, glorifying and praising God for all they had heard and seen . . . .

—Dan Benuska

Sunday After Christmas   *Worship/Stewardship*

LUKE 2:41-52

A Special Place for Unusual Persons

Being the father of a 12-year-old boy myself, I know boys and how often you can't find them when you want them. I can also tell you this, one of the least likely places I'd think of looking would be at church. No wonder Mary and Joseph were surprised at finding Jesus there. It takes a very unusual young man to stay behind there, to find his deepest joy and pleasure in being in the Father's house. In fact, no matter what their age, when we find someone like that we're surprised. So it was that a Nashville, Tennessee, newspaper carried a story about Mrs. Lila Craig, an 80-year-old woman, who hadn't missed attending church in 1,040 Sundays. The editor commented:

It makes one wonder what's the matter with Mrs. Craig. Doesn't it ever rain or snow in her home town on Sunday? Doesn't she ever have unexpected company? How is it that she doesn't go anywhere on Saturday night so that she's too tired to attend church on Sunday morning? Doesn't she ever beg off to attend family picnics or reunions, or to have headaches, colds, nervous spells, or read the Sunday newspaper? Hasn't she ever become angry at the ministry or had her feelings hurt by someone, and felt justified in staying home to hear a good sermon on television or the radio? What's the matter with Mrs. Craig, anyway?

—Religious News Service, adapted from *Pulpit Resource* Oxnard, CA: Vol. 8, No. 3
July, August, September 1980, p. 39
—Dan Benuska

Second Sunday After Christmas | *Incarnation*

JOHN 1:1-18

The Word with Skin On

The night was dark as pitch. The lightning cracked, the booming thunder made the house shake. "Dad, Dad," the little boy cried out. His father came in and leaned over the bed, "What's wrong?" he said. "I'm scared." "Don't worry, I'm in the room right next to you," the Father assured him. "I want someone in here," his little boy continued. "God is here, son, God is with you." "But Dad, I want someone with their skin on!" "The word became flesh and dwelt among us, full of grace and truth: we have beheld His glory . . ." that's the way John said it. On the facade of the United States Post Office in Washington, D.C., the words of Charles William Eliot are inscribed:

Carrier of news and knowledge, instrument of trade and commerce, promoter of mutual acquaintance among men and nations and hence of peace and good will.

Carrier of love and sympathy, messenger of friendship, consoler of the lonely, servant of the scattered family, enlarger of the public life.

Yes, words about the words we sent to one another. But for us, they are words about the Word.

—From *Bartlett's Quotations,* Emily Morison Beck, Editor, Boston:
Little, Brown, and Company. Fourteenth Edition, 1968.
—Dan Benuska

Epiphany of Our Lord | *Disclosure/Evidence*

MATTHEW 2:1-12

Let the Light Shine in Your Heart

Epiphany comes from a Greek word which means "to show, to reveal, to make manifest." Jesus is the light of the world, its hope, and its revealer. He brings to light the things hidden in darkness, He discloses the purposes of the heart. So it is by His light we see the hearts of the Magi—trusting and truthful, open and overflowing. So it is by His light we see the heart of Herod—devious and doubtful, hard and hateful. A prayer attributed to an African schoolgirl puts it directly and speaks the message of Epiphany:

O Thou, Great Chief, light a candle within my heart, that I may see what is therein and sweep the rubbish from Thy dwelling place!

—Materials adapted from *Mountain Trailways for Youth* compiled by
Mrs. Charles Cowman, Zondervan, Grand Rapids, MI, 1975
—Dan Benuska

The Baptism of Our Lord | *Baptism*
First Sunday After the Epiphany

LUKE 3:15-17, 21-22

Bridling the Runaway Horse

In *Creative Ministry,* Henri Nouwen tells the story of a perceptive encounter he had with a Buddhist monk.

While he looked straight into my eyes he said: "There was a man on a horse galloping swiftly along the road. An old farmer standing in the fields, seeing him pass by, called out, Hey, rider, where are you going? The rider turned around and shouted back, Don't ask me, just ask my horse!

The monk looked at me and said: "That is your condition. You are no longer master over your own destiny. You have lost control over the great powers that pull you forward toward an unknown direction. You have become a passive victim of an ongoing movement which you do not understand."

—*Creative Ministry*, Henri J. M. Nouwen, New York: Image Books, Doubleday, 1971, p. 3

Yes, that *is* our condition. We are not master over our own destiny. From the beginning to the end we are caught up in a power greater than our own. We cannot choose to be born, nor can we choose not to die. That is our condition, our dilemma, our bondage. Who will free us from it? The baptism of Jesus begins the song of freedom for us. He chooses the Jordan, He chooses the water, He chooses the baptism, He chooses the journey, He chooses the cross. He rides death out for us breaking its power and claim on us. He is its master. Yes, He chooses the destiny of the Father and knows His affirmation and blessing:

Thou art my beloved Son; with thee I am well pleased.

In our baptism, Jesus calls, "come follow, come, I claim you. Take My destiny as your own. Ride with Me and know the Father's plan for you. Ride with Me from baptism to the empty tomb. Ride with Me, I will hold you and sing the song of Easter and your victory."

—Dan Benuska

Second Sunday After the Epiphany

New Life/
Abundant Living

JOHN 2:1-11

The Good Scavenger

Sculptress Louise Nevelson, known for her sculptured collages made up of discarded fragments of wood and metal and machinery, was criticized as being "only a scavenger." "I take that as a compliment," she said. "Yes, it is true, I gather the castoffs and refuse of the world, but I put them together and give them new life." Isn't that what our Lord does? He takes the junk and leftovers of our life, He takes our weaknesses and failings, sorts through them, and puts us together with Him and makes something out of us. Can't we see the miracle of Cana repeated over and over again for us. He can take the thinnest, most insipid, most watery of lives and situations and give them new life, a life that has the fullness and sparkle of rich wine. The words from Song of Solomon spoken at another marriage feast, express all that our Lord wants to do for us:

My beloved speaks and says to me:
Arise my love, my fair one,
and come away;
for lo, the winter is past,
the rain is over and gone.
The flowers appear on the earth,
the time of singing has come,
and the voice of the turtledove
is heard in our land.
The fig tree puts forth its figs,
and the vines are in blossom;
they give forth fragrance.
Arise, my love, my fair one,
and come away.
—Song of Solomon 2:10-13

—Dan Benuska

Third Sunday After the Epiphany   *Love/New Life*

LUKE 4:14-21

What's Gotten into You?

"I just don't know what's gotten into you lately." Who of us hasn't spoken that about somebody. Who of us hasn't heard that spoken about us at some time or other. And usually, as we well know, it's not a compliment, because we've been unusually good but because we've been unusually nasty. How different it was for Jesus. What's gotten into Jesus? "The Spirit of the Lord is upon Me, because He has anointed Me to preach Good News to the poor, to proclaim release, to set at liberty, to proclaim the acceptable year of the Lord." What's gotten into Jesus proclaiming God's love to people like us. Yes, how different it is for us, when Jesus' love gets into us. The truth that change comes through love is revealed in a short vignette by Earnest Larsen, entitled: "You Try Love and I'll Try Ajax."

> Dear Mom,
>
> I have decided that you and not I are the casualty in the "Battle of the Bedroom." Yes, my bedroom is a mess. Yes, it's true you don't ask me to do much. But will wars end because I make my bed? Will all hunger in the world end because I hang up my clothes? With all the wonderful and terrible things happening in the world today, what does the condition of one bedroom matter?.
>
> Yes, I know that before the world can be put in order, each person must put his own little world in order. But dust doesn't bother my world. To put my world in order I need love, not Ajax cleaner. So, mom, I'll make you a deal. You use a little more love and I'll use a little more Ajax.
>
> —Kathy

—*Pulpit Resource*, Oxnard, CA: Vol. 8, No. 4, October, November, December 1980

—Dan Benuska

Fourth Sunday After the Epiphany   *Criticism/*
The Gracious Word

LUKE 4:21-32

Do You Have Any Complaints?

Donna, the Director of our Day School, has a large bright yellow poster on her wall. On it in big bold letters it says:

> Complaint Form
> Please write your complaint on the square below.
> Write legibly.

The space below, the space provided for complaints is a white, tiny half inch square. One day passing through her office I noticed that something had been written in that space. I was intrigued. Who could possible write a complaint, or at least a complaint that had any depth to it in that little space. Bending over and squinting I read it. It was direct and to the point.

> You don't love enough.

Needless to say I was taken back. Just a simple sentence but in reality, as we all know, the biggest and most persistent complaint that could be written over each of our lives. How different was the word spoken over Jesus: "And all spoke well of Him, and wondered at the gracious words which proceeded out of His mouth . . . ." Yes, thank God, that He writes another Word after the complaint form of our living. That Word is Jesus. It is a gracious Word, an astonishing Word, a Word of forgiveness and renewal.

—Dan Benuska

Fifth Sunday After the Epiphany
Rescue/Mission

LUKE 5:1-11

Voyage of the Rescued

The film, "Voyage of the Damned," is the true-life account of 937 Jewish refugees who were permitted by the Nazis to leave Germany aboard the S. S. St. Louis on May 13, 1939. The passengers believed they had bought aslyum in Cuba from the persecution that had begun in Germany. The boat trip was for them an escape from the concentration camps, a journey to freedom and a new life. Unknown to them, even before they had left Germany, it had been plotted and planned that they would be refused entry to Cuba. Upon arrival in Cuba, finding the door shut, they sought entry to the United States. While the major powers debated the political ramifications of the matter, the ship hovered uncertainly between the American coast and Cuba. As hope faded for the refugees, they became more and more desperate. Many attempted suicide, others considered overpowering the crew, risking the charge of mutiny rather then return to sure death in Germany. Finally with fuel running out, Captain Gustav Schroder had no other recourse but to head back to Germany. It was in every way the voyage of the damned.

The film is really a parable of our own life without Christ. Everyone sets out in life with high hopes. We board ship, we set sail, only to discover that the journey is a dead end. Before we leave port, our fate is decided. There will be pain, anxiety, suffering, and finally death. No amount of money or mental ability will keep us safe above and beyond death. No matter how we try, we cannot avoid it or detour around it. Sooner or later we would discover that we, too, are on the voyage of the damned. It is no accident that the church is pictured as a ship, a ship heading to the eternal port of peace. It is no accident that Jesus bids His disciples to enter the boat. Those that board do not turn their back on the world, they do not close their ears on the drowning cries of those around them, they become fishers of men. It is an astonishing task, a breathtaking opportunity.

—Dan Benuska

Transfiguration
Wake Up
Last Sunday After the Epiphany

LUKE 9:28-36

The Need for a Vision

Transfiguration is unimpressive! I don't mean unimpressive as a vision of Jesus' glory and true identity but unimpressive as a picture of Jesus' disciples. They just didn't seem to grasp it. There they are tired and dull, heavy with sleep. So typical of them, sleeping on the mountain, sleeping at Gethsemane Garden. Too tired to speak, they came down keeping silence, telling no one what they had seen. Sleeping through significant moments, living in a daze is typical of those disciples and at times typical of us too. Several years ago, on a winters trip back to Ohio, I went to the little restaurant that served as the gathering place for some of my old high school classmates. In a corner booth, I found Terry sitting alone. "Where's the rest of the guys?" I said. "Dead," Terry replied, "all three of them are dead! Didn't you read about it? It made national news. You know them, it was to be a lark, another good time, a continuation of Friday night's party. They hired a plane to do some skydiving early the next morning. They parachuted out over Lake Erie by mistake." Then I recalled reading about the event. No names had been mentioned in the article, so I never connected it with anyone I knew. They had gone up at Sandusky Airport in a cold, drizzling fog. The plane had gotten off course and one by one had dropped them into the freezing water and ice of Lake Erie. "You know what bothers me most," Terry continued, "they died like they

73

lived—in a fog, never knowing where they were or where they were going!" Jesus doesn't want any of us to die or live in a fog. He wants to take us to a high mountain apart. He wants to give us a vision. He doesn't want us to sleep through it. Wake up, look, listen, before it's too late.

—Dan Benuska

First Sunday in Lent   *Temptation*

LUKE 4:1-13

Christ's Temptations Same as Ours

At first glance the temptations of Jesus seem strange. They are so unlike our temptations to take things, use people, and ignore God. They seem so odd. Make bread out of stones? Leap from the temple? Worship Satan to gain the world? They seem almost silly.

Yet the temptations are ours. We delude ourselves and empower Satan if we make him into a costumed prankster bent on getting us to do wrong. Doing wrong comes easy to us—we need no help there.

Satan is interested in what we think, what we believe about ourselves and God.

Look at Satan. What is he saying? "If You are the Son of God . . . If You are . . . . If You really think You are—then can You not prove Your power through a self-serving miracle? Can You not prove God's care by leaping from the temple? Can You not gain the world my way? If You are . . ."

How often have we heard his words in ourselves. "If you are the child of God would you act that way—would you not be able to overcome your weaknesses, do the good you intended, straighten yourself out? Would God treat you that way? If you are? Are you really? Really a child of God?"

—Theodore W. Schroeder

Second Sunday in Lent   *Comfort*

LUKE 13:31-35

The Weeping King

In times of trouble there is something comforting about the Jesus of the Book of Revelation. As a victorious warrior He stands at the throne of God grasping the future firmly in His hands and accepting the adulation of the spiritual and physical world.

But when we are caught in sin, torn by doubt, and stranded a million faith miles from the Savior who died for us, there is no more comforting view of Jesus than to see Him bent over His hands and weeping over a rebellious people who would not come when He called and called and called again.

We need a Savior who can rule the world. But more, we need a Savior/Friend who loves us enough to weep over us and call us again and again when we stray.

—Theodore W. Schroeder

Third Sunday in Lent   *Impenitence*

LUKE 13:1-9

The Fatal Fascination

The Frenchman, J. Henri Fabre, wrote about a particular bee-eating wasp, the Philanthus. It had killed a honeybee. To extract the honey, the wasp squeezes its crop to make her disgorge the delicious syrup, which she drinks by licking the tongue which her unfortunate victim, in her death agony, sticks out of her mouth at full length. At the moment of some such horrible banquet, I have seen the wasp, with her prey, seized by the Mantis—the bandit was rifled by another bandit. And here is an awful detail: while the Mantis held her transfixed under the points of the double saw and was already munching her belly, the wasp continued to lick the honey of her bee, unable to relinquish the delicious food even amid the terrors of death.

—Quoted in *The Lutheran* by Pastor A. W. Podlich, October 29, 1979
—Theodore W. Schroeder

Fourth Sunday in Lent   *Temptation*

LUKE 15:1-3

"Lead Us Not into Temptation"

Temptation may be seen positively as a trial, negatively as a seduction. But most of all it has the positive-negative polarity in mind: it appeals to man's faith or nonfaith. Petty vices are not the main distractions. The greatest saints are known to have noticed pretty girls; reasonably ethical prophets have been known to take a nip. But both saints and prophets were in the orbit of real temptation in those or other acts because the Christ in them was being assaulted by His one great enemy . . . .

What is clear, then, is that temptation is not removed but accented for the Christian . . . .

A good translation of these words could be, "Snatch us not away in the hour of temptation." For the semifinal, penultimate forms of temptation are related to the final, the ultimate forms. . . . God is not to abandon His hidden flock and its members in the evil hours of their existence. Family, finance, success, self-dignity, keeping schedules: all these can be penultimate distractions. But in the end they are always part of a big distraction: the death of the spiritual life, hell made visible. Against this, God is asked to wage war. . . .

The final victory is assured. God did not abandon Jesus Christ. The one who prays this prayer is identified with Christ in the middle of the world. He still has enemies, an enemy: but prayer can resist him and drive him back.

—Martin Marty, *The Hidden Discipline* St. Louis: Concordia, 1974, pp. 83—85
—Theodore W. Schroeder

Fifth Sunday in Lent   *Evil to Good*

LUKE 20:9-19

Evil Turned to Good

Edwin E. Roberson was flattened by a bolt of lightning and was out for 20 minutes. When he came to, he could "hear like a kid" even though his hearing aid had been burned out by the blast. His eyes had been so bad he had no reflex to light. Now he is 20/20. And after being bald for 35 years he now sports a thick head of hair.

—"Lightning Struck" by Dean Haran, *Science Digest*, May, 1981
—Theodore W. Schroeder

Sunday of the Passion   *Sacrifice*
Palm Sunday

LUKE 22:1—23: 56 OR LUKE 23:1-49

Against All Odds

In a *Newsweek* article entitled "Where Have All the Heroes Gone?" Pete Axheim tells the story of James Bonneham at the Alamo. While under siege, he slipped through the enemy lines and rode ninety miles to the army garrison at Goliad and asked for reinforcements. The commander there said that he had none to send. Knowing the Alamo was doomed, James Bonneham made his way back to join the others in the Alamo and die there. To Pete Axheim, James Bonneham was a greater hero than the others who died in the Alamo because he had a choice. He could have saved himself, but he went back knowing it would mean his demise. He could not live staying away, even if he would not live going back. Yes, that is the hero aspect. Against all odds, they do what they have to do.

He came into the world He made, came back for us knowing it would mean His demise. Against all odds—when all others would give up on us, still He loves us and claims us. Yes, against all odds, we are His, and nothing will separate us from Him.

—Dan Benuska

Maundy Thursday   *Forgiveness*

LUKE 22:7-10

God Does Not Excuse; He Forgives

We tend to use the words "excuse" and "forgive" as synonyms. They are not.

While we might say "forgive me" when we bump someone accidentally, we would not ask a person we have greatly injured to "excuse" us.

While drunk, a man ran down and killed a child. Crushed with remorse he sought out the parents of the child.

"Can you ever forgive me?" he asked.

The father replied, "I will never be able to excuse what you did, but I will seek God's help to forgive you."

How we cheapen God's act in Christ when we imply that God excuses sin. How pointless the death of Jesus if God's response to our guilt is "It's all right; it doesn't matter; I excuse you."

God does not excuse. He forgives.

—Theodore W. Schroeder

Good Friday   *Man/Redemption*

JOHN 18:1—19:42 OR JOHN 19:17-30

"What Is Man?"

"What is man that Thou art mindful of him?"—Psalm 8:4

"Man is a biped without feathers."—Plato

"Man is a social animal."—Seneca

"Man is the only animal that blushes—or needs to."—Mark Twain

"Man is an intelligence in service to his organs."—Huxley

The physicist: A human being is an entropy decreaser.

The chemist: A human being is a product of the carbon atom.

The biochemist: A human being is a nucleic acid/enzyme interaction.

The biologist: A human being is a cell conglomerate.

But in the crucifixion I know I am a child of God, redeemed by the sacrifice of the Son of God and of eternal value to Him.

—Based on "Identifying Ourselves" by Isaac Asimov, *Science Digest* May 1981
—Theodore W. Schroeder

The Resurrection of Our Lord

LUKE 24:1-11 OR JOHN 20:1-9

The Easter Dandelion

The lily is a most familiar Easter object. And indeed, the white lily reminds us of the brightness and joy of the event, and its trumpet shape recalls the angel's announcement. But the lily is not really an Easter flower. It must be fooled into blooming in spring. And it is a rather fragile flower, easily damaged and short-lived; its remarkable bloom soon fades and falls away.

There is another flower more suited to be the symbol of the resurrection. It too recalls the bright Easter event with its sunny yellow face. But unlike the lily the dandelion is a true resurrection flower. It is almost indestructible. Blooming in spring it can hardly be denied its place in the lawn. Pulled out by the root, the flower will reroot itself while the broken root will grow a new flower. It is so determined to grow that it will move rocks, asphalt, and even cement to reach the light of day.

The lily might recall some of the beauty of the Easter event, but the dandelion certainly proclaims the undeniable victory of God's Christ who could not be overcome, even by death itself.

—Theodore W. Schroeder

The Resurrection of Our Lord

LUKE 24:1-11 OR JOHN 20:1-9

The Regenerative Starfish

All starfish have some ability to regenerate new parts after injury. Most can grow a new arm when it is severed. The severed arm of some species such as *Astras Rubens* can regenerate into a whole new animal if a part of the central disk (mouth and digestive organs) remains attached. The Linchia don't even need a piece of the disk but can regenerate completely from only a small portion of one arm.

Truly, if you try to rid yourself of starfish by cutting them up, you may well find yourself up to your ears in starfish.

—*Science Digest* May 1981
—Theodore W. Schroeder

Second Sunday of Easter

JOHN 20:19-31

Hard to Believe

It's very difficult for a man to believe that God is gracious to him. The human heart can't grasp this. What happened in my case? I was once terrified by the sacrament which Dr. Staupitz carried in a procession in Eisleben on the feast of Corpus Christi. I went along in the procession and wore the dress of a priest. Afterward I made confession to Dr. Staupitz, and he said to me, "Your thought is not of Christ." With this word he comforted me well. This is the way we are. Christ offers Himself to us together with the forgiveness of sins, and yet we flee from His face.

This also happened to me as a boy in my homeland when we sang in order to gather sausages. A townsman jokingly cried out, "What are you boys up to? May this or that evil overtake you!" At the same time he ran toward us with two sausages. With my companion I took to my feet and ran away from the man who was offering his gift. This is precisely what happens to us in our relation to God. He gave us Christ with all his gifts, and yet we flee from him and regard him as our judge.

—Martin Luther, *Luther's Works,* American Edition (St. Louis: Concordia Publishing House, Vols. 1—30; Philadelphia: Fortress Press, Vols. 31—54) Vol. 54, Table Talk, p. 19.

Third Sunday of Easter   *Miracles*

JOHN 21:1-14

Missed Miracles

The trouble with casting out the net is that Jesus might fill it.
Then what?
We'll have to break our back to haul in the fish, spend half the night cleaning and sorting the fish, and work for hours repairing the nets torn by the size of the catch.
How much easier to stay on the shore, dipnet a minnow or two, and rest.
How many drafts of miracles have we missed because we were dipnetting minnows on the beach instead of casting out nets of faith into the sea?

—Theodore W. Schroeder

Fourth Sunday of Easter   *Faith*

JOHN 10:22-30

Planning by Faith

Englishman James Bryce was amazed as he attended the cornerstone laying for the new capitol building for the Territory (later to become states) of Dakota. While the town was brightly decorated for the occasion, the actual stone was set on a knoll almost a mile from town.
"Do you plan to surround the building in a park?" asked the visitor.
"By no means," he was told. "This will be the center of town. This is the direction the town will grow."

—From *American Heritage,* "Lord Bryce" by Louis Auchincloss, April/May 1981
—Theodore W. Schroeder

Fifth Sunday of Easter   *Servanthood*

JOHN 13:31-35

"You Have Done It unto Me"

The man lay in the alley near death from the savage beating he had suffered. The ruffians who had attacked him for his money were gone.
Just as he felt himself losing consciousness, he saw the amber streetlight surround the head of a man bending over him.
He awoke in the hospital. The nurse told him that the man who had brought him in wanted to see him.
"I want to thank you," muttered the attack victim from his bed.
"It was nothing," came the reply.
"You know—it's funny. But when you came to help me out there in that dim light, I thought you were Jesus.
"You know," replied the visitor, "When I moved toward your cry in the alley, I thought you were Jesus."

—Theodore W. Schroeder

Sixth Sunday of Easter   *Contentment*

JOHN 14:23-29

Jelly Bread—or Daily Bread

"Give us this day our jelly bread," my brother used to pray. And he was not far from what we'd all like to pray.

Bread is all right when you don't have anything else, but it sure tastes a lot better with some jelly on it. Then, of course, we wouldn't mind some soup to wash it down with. And perhaps some meat and potatoes to go with it. Well, why not a banquet? After all we deserve it. Some of the people of the world seem to have everything. We certainly should have a break or two now and then.

Lord, we are grateful for the bread, but couldn't You make it cake instead?

—Theodore W. Schroeder

The Ascension of our Lord   *Repentance/Forgiveness*

LUKE 24:44-53

"Satisfied with yourself?"

"In your churches I too often found the challenge for repentance missing from the preacher's message. The general tendency was to treat all members of the congregation *eo ipso* as Christians who did not need any basic change in their lives. Often after the service I had the somewhat sorry feeling that everybody was going home very satisfied with the good service and the fine sermon but nobody was dissatisfied with himself. If I had to choose a text for a sermon to be preached in your churches, I would take Luther's first thesis: 'When our Lord Jesus said "Repent ye," He meant that the whole life of the believer should be one of repentance.'"

—From *The National Lutheran,* "A Finnish Pastor Looks at American Lutheranism," March 1948

Seventh Sunday of Easter   *Trust*

JOHN 17:20-26

How Trustworthy Is Man?

Today our nation has squadrons of missiles deep in the ground, aimed, and ready to go off. The greatest problem in devising this defensive system, however, was insuring that it would be triggered only when necessary.

So at the end of a potential countdown, there are two men, neither of which can fire the missiles alone. They work together but are separated by a wall of bulletproof glass. We are afraid that one person could misuse the powerful weapons.

We commend the integrity of those serving our country in the Armed Forces. But will we ever be able to *fully* trust another human being?

—Donald L. Deffner

The Day of Pentecost   *Holy Spirit*

JOHN 15:26-27; 16:4b-11

The Neglected Waiting Bench

On the way to church we keep passing a bench that was originally placed there with good intentions. People waiting for the bus could sit there comfortably.

For the longest time, however, it has been tilted off its base; and falling apart. Tall grass and weeds are growing around it. Nevertheless you can still read the fading ad someone had painted on its back. But no one uses the bench anymore. It is decrepit and just waiting to be hauled away.

It's easy to imagine how it got there in the first place. Someone got the bright idea that a need would be served by a waiting bench at the bus stop, and that someone would be willing to pay for it.

But the mistake was in not making provisions for the bench's upkeep. It was as though everyone thought that since it was made and paid for and erected, it would somehow take care of itself.

When we got to church, I thought, "How wise of God not to do the same with the church He created at Pentecost!" He made it for the spiritual need of the human race. It cost Him much to provide it for everyone, and He inscribed it with a message. But He also provided for its maintenance! He gave His Spirit to keep it in good repair, to keep it functioning, to protect it from deterioration, to keep it solid on its foundation, and to keep the message clear and attractive.

—J. J. Vajda

The Holy Trinity   *Changeless Truth*
First Sunday After Pentecost

JOHN 16:12-15

A Changeless Christ

In ancient Greek philosophy, there was a character by the name of Cratylus. Now the master of Cratylus was Heraclitus; and he philosophized that you could not step into the same river twice; for in the process of constant flowing its substance would have changed. Now Cratylus went one step further, and said that you couldn't even step into the same river once, since by the time you had stepped into it, it would not be the same river into which you had decided to step.

And if we carried this still further, we would have to conclude that you couldn't even say anything about stepping into a river, for by the time you had finished the statement, the river which you had in mind wouldn't even be there. And the final conclusions we would have to draw from such a philosophy would be that you would simply have to scurry around as fast as possible and rapidly point to things before they had changed into something else.—Adapted from T. A. Kantonen, *The Message of the Church to the World of Today,* Minneapolis: Augsburg, 1941, p. 3.

The world is filled with change today. And the church must be aware of these changes, and how to address its message to contemporary hearers. But no matter how much the world changes, our blessed Lord Jesus Christ, the Head of the church, never changes. "He is the same yesterday, and today, and forever." He is the "changeless Christ for a changing world."

—Donald L. Deffner

Second Sunday After Pentecost   *Faith*

LUKE 7:1-10

Reach Out—Have No Fear

A group of workers were hiding behind a protective wall as a dynamite fuse burned itself towards an old building which was to be demolished. Suddenly a 3-year-old child appeared walking towards the building.

80

The workmen yelled to the child to come back, but this only terrified the child more, and it walked faster towards the death-filled building.

All at once the child's mother appeared. She had been searching for her child and quickly saw the infant, the building, and the dynamite fuse.

Filled with fear, but with the alertness of a mother saving her child, she opened her arms, and cried from her heart: "Come to me, my darling."

Instantly, with eager, pattering feet and little arms opened to her arms, the girl ran back from the building and did not stop until she was clasped in her mother's bosom.

This trust and love of a child for its parents is the childlike dependency we are called to have towards God.

"Take heart," He calls out to us. "It is I; have no fear."

—Donald L. Deffner

Third Sunday After Pentecost   *Jesus' Love*

LUKE 7:11-17

The Most Profound Statement

A seminary student once asked the renowned theologian Karl Barth: "What is the most profound statement you have ever heard?"

Barth replied: "Jesus loves me, this I know. For the Bible tells me so."

—Donald L. Deffner

Fourth Sunday After Pentecost   *Forgiveness*

LUKE 7:36-50

Forgiveness, Not Just Love

"I know a married couple who had a real squabble, and the husband hurt his wife's feelings. After a few tense moments the husband told his wife, 'I love you.' His wife immediately responded, 'Love isn't going to solve all our problems!' And then the husband confessed, 'Honey, I'm sorry; will you forgive me?'"

—Donald L. Deffner

Fifth Sunday After Pentecost   *Self-Denial*

LUKE 9:18-24

"Out With the Tooth!"

Christ says, "Give me *all*. I don't want so much of your money and so much of your work—I want *you*. I have not come to torment your natural self, but to kill it. No half-measures are any good. I don't want to cut off a branch here and a branch there, I want to have the whole tree down. I don't want to drill the tooth, or crown it, or stop it, but to have it out. Hand over the whole natural self. . . . I will give you a new self instead. In fact I will give you myself, my own will shall become yours."

—C. S. Lewis, *Beyond Personality,* New York: Macmillan, 1964, p. 40

Sixth Sunday After Pentecost   *Follow Me*

LUKE 9:51-62

The Hero Never Appeared

Nathaniel Hawthorne once scratched a story idea in one of his notebooks—just this phrase: "Idea for a story—a story in which the principle character never appeared!" Among others who have used the idea is Samuel Beckett, the author of the well-known play *Waiting for Godot.*

Many a person's life follows this same plot. It is a story in which the chief character never appeared. To use J. B. Phillips' metaphor, the linotyper had it all set, but when he was out to lunch, some madman came in and disarranged all the type. In a sense, God has a master plan for our lives; we frustrate the plan, and the person He wanted us to be never appears.

—Donald L. Deffner, et. al., *Meditations for College Students*
(St. Louis: Concordia Publishing House, 1961). p. 15.

Seventh Sunday After Pentecost   *Witnessing for Christ*

LUKE 10:1-12, 16

A Loving God

A Christian missionary to New Guinea recounts how earlier missionaries had frightened the natives by throwing sweet potatoes into a raging fire and saying: "That's the way you will burn in God's hell if you don't believe in and worship Him." Many natives joined the church, but their "conversion" did not last.

This missionary rather began with the story of a *loving* God and a *good* creation that mankind had disrupted. Then later the story of Calvary and Christ's loving death for man's sin was told.

—Donald L. Deffner

Eighth Sunday After Pentecost   *Commitment/Service*

LUKE 10:25-37

"Let Someone Else do it . . ."

The church was saddened to learn of the death this week of one of our church's most valuable members. Someone Else.

Someone Else's passing creates a vacancy that will be difficult to fill. Someone Else has been with us for many years. Someone Else did far more than a normal person's share of the work. Whenever there was a job to do, a class to teach, or a meeting to attend, one name was on everyone's list: "Let Someone Else do it."

It was common knowledge that Someone Else was among the largest givers in the church. Whenever there was a financial need, everyone just assumed Someone Else would make up the difference. Someone Else was a wonderful person—sometimes appearing superhuman, but a person can only do so much. Were the truth known, everybody expected too much of Someone Else.

Now Someone Else is gone! We wonder what we are going to do. Someone Else left a wonderful example to follow, but WHO is going to do the things Someone Else did? When you are asked to help, REMEMBER—we can't depend on Someone Else!

—Contribution of Bobbie Mechler to the Trinity Lutheran Church *Newsletter,*
Walnut Creek, CA, January 1979.

Ninth Sunday After Pentecost   *Growing—in the Word*

LUKE 10:38-42

"No Level Ground"

Perhaps you have heard of parents who have a crippled or mentally retarded child, who did not realize the child's condition at first. There were the early days when the parents laughed at the helplessness of the child, its stumbling efforts to speak, its lack of coordination and self-control. But then came the days when the growth which was expected did not come, and the parents slowly—and painfully—realized that the child was not maturing in a normal way.

How helpful it would be if we were more concerned about spiritual atrophy with the same sorrow and dismay! The trouble is we often think we are "holding our own" as far as the Christian faith is concerned, whereas all we may have left is a sterile, intellectual assent to certain doctrines being true!—which is not the living *relationship* with God which is the Christian faith.

There is no "level ground" as far as Christianity is concerned. One is either ascending or descending—growing . . . or stagnating.

—*The Doctrine in the Liturgy,* St. Louis, Concordia Seminary Print Shop, 1960
—Donald L. Deffner

Tenth Sunday After Pentecost   *God's Good Gifts*

LUKE 11:1-13

The Water and the Word

Helen Keller's nurse had tried everything to get her to see the relationship between words and objects. But Helen could not hear or see, and did not get the connection.

Then one day, Helen felt the cool water coming out of the pump, and delighted in its cool touch. Immediately her teacher started to spell out W-A-T-E-R to Helen by touch. Amazingly, for the first time the concept formed in her brain—the connection between the water, the word, and the cool liquid flowing onto her hand. And then the whole world opened to her because other names and words could be transmitted to her understanding.

When we see the relationship between our baptism and our life and the gifts it offers through Christ, the whole world of heaven and earth is opened to us.

—Donald L. Deffner

Eleventh Sunday After Pentecost   *Materialism*

LUKE 12:13-21

"Go Easy, Lord"

"Benevolent and easy-going Father: I have occasionally been guilty of error of judgment.... But, I have done the best I could under the circumstances ... and I am glad to think that I am fairly normal. I beg you, O Lord, deal lightly with my infrequent lapses. Be your own sweet self with me because nobody's perfect! According to the unlimited tolerance which I have a right to expect from You. And please remain my indulgent parent, that I may hereafter continue to live a harmless and happy life and keep my self-respect."

—David Head, *He Sent Leanness,* New York: Macmillan, 1959, p. 19

Twelfth Sunday After Pentecost   *Planning*

LUKE 12:23-40

It is a bit surprising to find that some persons question whether we have a right to plan. They interpret Jesus' "take no thought for tomorrow," seriously. "Are we playing God when we try to control the future? Don't planners manipulate people and events so that things come out as they planned?" they ask.

I've also known people who never promise to do something or go somewhere in the future without adding the phrase, "God willing (Deo volente)." In this way they remind themselves of their own limited control over tomorrow.

Bonhoeffer says that God has given man the power to decide. We are afraid to stretch every skill we have been given so that we can share in the creation of a better world. Yet, in so doing we are not pushing God farther out to the periphery of our lives, we are recognizing Him as the center and source of our power. To plan is to trust that God will give us a tomorrow, and Jesus tells us here that tomorrow does include His coming again.

—Eugene E. Schmidt

Thirteenth Sunday After Pentecost   *The Word*

LUKE 12:49-53

Winston Churchill at the height of World War II had a counter-question to those who asked, "What are we fighting for?" He said, "Stop fighting and you'll soon find out." Jesus' word to us is a reminder that when the church preaches the Word, conflict will arise even amongst friends. But, if we stop preaching the Word in order to avoid this conflict, "we'll soon find out why." We must follow God's command to preach the word.

—Eugene E. Schmidt

Fourteenth Sunday After Pentecost   *Discipleship*

LUKE 13:22-30

Discipleship always denotes a personal relationship. In the Old Testament and in the Greek world disciples selected their own rabbis or teachers to learn their philosophy or teachings. When Jesus says, "I do not know you," He is emphasizing that discipleship is a relationship defined as a follower of Jesus.

The apostles refrained from using the word "disciple" in their epistles, no doubt because in the Greek world this would place greater emphasis on the teachings of Jesus than on the person of Jesus.

—Walter Stuenkel

Fifteenth Sunday After Pentecost   *Humility*

LUKE 14:1, 7-14

There is a difference between loving yourself and being in love with yourself. A person who loves himself as God loves him, a poor miserable sinner redeemed by Christ, cannot give in to pride. A person who is *in love with himself* will push himself in front of others.

—Albert C. Burroughs

Sixteenth Sunday After Pentecost   *Discipleship*

LUKE 14:25-33

This passage from Luke's gospel is uncompromising. What is it that God wants of us? Hans Küng has these thoughts about what is expected. "Jesus expects a different new person: a radically changed awareness, a fundamentally different attitude, a completely new orientation in thought and action. The meaning now becomes clear of a term, which is of central importance, 'Metanoia' (conversion), or as it was formerly misleadingly translated, 'repentance.' It is not a question of doing penance externally in sackcloth and ashes. It is not an intellectually determined or strongly emotional religious experience. It is a change of will, an awareness change from the roots upwards, a new basis attitude, a different scale of values. That is 'Metanoia,' taking up one's cross."

—Hans Küng, *Being a Christian,* New York: Doubleday & Co. 1976

Seventeenth Sunday After Pentecost   *Lost*

LUKE 15:1-10

Out on the farm I met the farmer walking down the lane carrying a half-grown sheep. He greeted me, "Have to look after the stray." I asked, "How do they get lost?" "They just nibble themselves lost," he answered; "they just keep their heads down and just wander from one green patch to another. Sometimes they come to a hole in the fence, but they never find the hole to get back in again."

This parable repeats itself in our lives. We eat ourselves lost, we work ourselves lost. We don't look up. We wander from one wish or mirage to another. We get our heads in the pits, we can't see the way back in again. Thank God for the Good Shepherd who always comes to seek and to save the lost.

—Eugene E. Schmidt

Eighteenth Sunday After Pentecost   *Faithfulness*

LUKE 16:1-13

Booker T. Washington is known to have said when facing difficult times, "What are the advantages of the disadvantages?" We have the disadvantage of living in a fallen world. Jesus here indicates that His followers will seek the advantages of the disadvantage of living in a fallen world to His glory.

—Eugene E. Schmidt

Nineteenth Sunday After Pentecost   *The Word*

LUKE 16:19-31

Martin Franzmann, former professor at Concordia Seminary, St. Louis, Missouri, entitled a sermon on the Centurion, "A Man Who Went Home with Only a Word in His Pocket."

"When we come right down to it all the church really has is the Word and the Sacraments. The spectacular, the publicity, the dramatic is all overshadowed by the 'Strong Word' which 'cleaves the darkness.'"

—Martin Franzmann

Twentieth Sunday After Pentecost   *The Faith*

LUKE 17:1-10

"Here is an eyeopener for some. Like the disciples many of us are eager for a larger portion of faith. The faith to guide people aright, faith to forgive, faith to serve just for the privilege. As we face the tough issues of life, we cry out for more faith. No one can honestly say, "I have all the faith in the world." If we really have faith, do we need more? Jesus here corrects the disciples' desire for more faith. He says the quality or degree of faith does not matter. It is sufficient just to have faith. The parable of the mustard seed emphasizes that the smallest amount of faith can do wonders. The admonition of this sermon is 'have faith,' not 'have more faith.'"

—John R. Brokhoff, *Lectionary Preaching*, Lima, OH: C.S.S. Publishing Co., n.a., p. 204

Twenty-First Sunday After Pentecost   *Gratitude*

LUKE 17:11-19

Hans Selye describes two kinds of stress in human behavior as distress and eustress. Distress is destructive. Eustress is that elixir of life that gives us vitality and a spring to our step. Dr. Selye presented his findings on stress in his monumental landmark book, *The Stress of Life*. Eustress, he writes, is found among those who have an attitude of gratitude, who live life thankfully. This truth is also found in this text and throughout the sacred Scriptures.

—Eugene E. Schmidt

Twenty-Second Sunday After Pentecost   *Perseverance*

LUKE 18:1-8a

Calbraith Perry Rogers is the little known aviator who in 1911 completed the first coast to coast crossing of the United States in an airplane. Roger's plane was a Wright Ex Biplane. He took off from Sheepshead Bay, Long Island, N.Y., on Sept. 17, 1911, and landed in Pasadena, Calif., on Nov. 5, 1911. He made his ultimate goal of Long Beach, Calif., one month later.

It took 49 days to make the trip. His time in the air was 3 days, 10 hours, 14 minutes. Along the way he crashed 39 times and made 30 other unscheduled stops. The only parts of the original plane that were left and completed his venture were a vertical rudder and the drip pan. All he had for the trip was himself and the ability to fly. When you come right down to it, this is a very apt analogy about life. All we really have is God and His promise to us!

—From TEAM-LEA, Department & Directors of Christian Education

Reformation   *Freedom Is*

JOHN 8:31-36

As the naturally fortified hill of Masada near the shore of the Dead Sea in Palestine is a symbol of death for freedom's sake for the people of Israel, so the Alamo in San Antonio is a symbol of death for freedom's sake for the citizens of America. The Alamo is a symbol of freedom because Colonel William Barret Travis drew a line on the ground before his battle weary men and said in a voice trembling with emotion, "Those prepared to give their lives in freedom's cause come over to me."

Jesus here also draws a line for us between servanthood and slavery and calls us to freedom so that we might know the truth in Him. Slavery is servitude to a master who seeks only his own good. Servanthood is the freedom of serving a master who sought our good by dying on the cross for us. Our battle cry is "justified by grace." By that act of love and mercy we were freed for servanthood.

—Eugene E. Schmidt

Third-Last Sunday of the Church Year

Response to the Second Coming

LUKE 17:20-30

People respond to life either as actors, reactors, or procrastinators. Here our Lord describes these three kinds of people in their reaction to the promise of His second coming.

The procrastinators are oblivious to the reality of the Word of God and the end of time and so keep on wining and dining. The reactors follow every announcement of the coming of a kingdom. The actors have found the Christ, act out their Christian lives, and in full confidence believe that when the end comes the Prince of Peace whom they know now will be present.

—Eugene E. Schmidt

Second-Last Sunday in the Church Year

Fear of Failure

LUKE 19:11-27

The fear of doing something wrong or the fear of the future immobilizes many people. The unfortunate man in this parable is that kind of person. Jesus tells us that the greatest mistake in life is to do nothing with our lives and thus supposedly make no mistakes. This parable endorses the saying, "I would rather try something great and fail than do nothing and succeed." Our Lord suggests that we try bold things for Him in spite of the fear of making mistakes. In fact He encourages us to follow in the footsteps of the Savior and to invest our moments, our energies, and our lives with confidence in glorifying His name.

—Eugene E. Schmidt

Last Sunday in the Church Year
Sunday of the Fulfillment

Final Seconds

LUKE 12:42-48

The championship game of the 1982 NCAA basketball tournament was a classic showdown between North Carolina and Georgetown University. With only a few seconds to go a player from Georgetown University, whose team at the moment was losing by one point, passed the ball to a North Carolina player, who controlled it long enough to determine the outcome. Then the buzzer sounded to end the game. It spelled victory for North Carolina.

How many of us have had the fear that before the trumpet sounds at the end of time we may make a certain wrong move that will lose the game of life in Christ for us?

Here our Lord again explains that what really counts is faithfulness: full of faith in Him and His forgiving love and grace, and faithfulness in our Christian responsibilities. So Christ counts not whether we made the right move at the last second. He knows we are sinners. He knows also that we are living in His forgiveness and love, and that is great. That's the joy of this text.

—Eugene E. Schmidt

Index of Scripture Texts

Index of Topics

Add Your Own

Add Your Own

Add Your Own

Add Your Own

Add Your Own

Add Your Own